FAMILY FUN
and
ACTIVITIES

by

Margaret E. Mulac

Illustrated by Julianne

Harper & Brothers, Publishers, New York

FAMILY FUN AND ACTIVITIES

Copyright © 1958 by Margaret E. Mulac

Printed in the United States of America

FIRST EDITION

D–H

Library of Congress catalog card number: 58-6162

This book is affectionately dedicated to the members of my family, of which it has always been fun to be a part: Dorothy and Paul Gross, Carol and Chris Hoffmann and Christine Mulac, and to their children, Julianne, Paul James, Peter Martin and John Edwin Gross, Michael James Hoffmann and Jeanne Katherine Mulac, and to my parents and brother, Anna M. Mulac, James M. Mulac and Edwin F. Mulac, whose contributions to happy family living still glow brightly in the memories of us all.

Contents

Contents

Acknowledgments

Acknowledgment is made with gratitude to these individuals and families who consciously or unknowingly have made contributions to this book: Kenneth Bendig, Jeannette Earhart, Robert Howell, Carol Hoffmann, Helen L. Jewitt, Mae McLaren, Christine Mulac, Dorcas Reece, Betty and Howard Sprague, Carl and Violet Peterson, and to all the families with whom the author has had the fun of working and playing. Special recognition is due the members of the 1957 Recreation Class of the Graduate School of Western Reserve University and to Marian S. Holmes, whose buoyancy, creativeness and spontaneity are always a source of inspiration.

Foreword

This book is devoted to families—how they may work together, play together, learn together and share together the blessings of family life. It is not always the parents who give and not only the children who receive. Each has something to give to the other that is precious beyond price. From parents to children flow tenderness, love, the wisdom of experience, security, everyday needs of food, shelter and clothing, protection, discipline, sacrifice of self. The children, in return, give love that is close to worship, and all the wonderful qualities of youth—wonderment, buoyancy, exuberance, freshness, eagerness—those qualities of life which become shorter and shorter in supply in adults unless they renew them constantly at the fountains of youth.

Good family life is *made* in the home, it cannot be purchased in the market place. Good family life is people living together, playing and working together, loving one another, sacrificing for each other, fighting for each other, standing together in matters of principle, comforting each other, rejoicing together, praying and worshiping together, believing in each other. It is sharing of the lean as well as the fat years. It is protecting the weak in the family and not exploiting the strong. Good family life is based on human values, and not material possessions. Even with a meager supply of worldly goods the good family life may exist. A vast fortune cannot buy a good family life if the necessary human qualities are lacking.

Often when a teen-ager has been apprehended for some misdemeanor, the newspaper report will read "The boy came from a better home." "Better home" as applied here is a misnomer. What the reporter means is that the boy came from a better house—one belonging to a family in a high-income bracket living in a choice residential district. A home is not necessarily a better home because of its location, its initial cost or its present value. It may not be so good a home as one located in a modest neighborhood. It is not the type of house or the section of town in which it is located which makes it a poor or a good home.

No house is a home until people are living in it. The kind of life that is maintained in the house is what makes it a poor or a good home.

No home where each member goes his own way, where there is no mutual respect, where communication between members is lacking, where love does not abide could ever be termed a good home regardless of how many deluxe model cars filled the garage or how expensive the furnishings. On the other hand, where there are love, laughter and joyous living within its walls, any house, however humble its exterior or its furnishings is truly a better home. There is a tendency to put great emphasis on *things* in determining what makes a good life. Parents are subjected to terrific pressures from without which drive them to attempt to keep up with or surpass the Joneses. Unless people learn to stand firm against such pressures, they find themselves running faster and faster in the attempt to amass wealth. They learn too late that this is a poor substitute for the real factors of life which make living worthwhile.

It is not how much money one has or how expensive his possessions that is important. What is important is whether these possessions make the individual happy. It does not necessarily follow that a family with an income of a hundred thousand dollars per year is ten times happier than one with a ten-thousand-dollar income or twenty times more contented than the family which struggles along on five thousand.

The basis for distinguishing between the real and false value often lies within our own scope of experience. What are the happiest memories of our childhood? Are they centered around possessions or around incidents which involve those we loved—our parents, brothers and sisters, grandparents, aunts and uncles?

We find ourselves remembering the family picnics where parents and grandparents, uncles, aunts and cousins shared good food, played games together and played pranks on each other. Do we remember what kind of china was used at the picnic or whether or not the car we drove to the picnic grounds was as luxurious a model as our neighbors'? Not so. We remember instead the prankster uncle who rubbed Limburger cheese under the dainty aunt's nose. We recall the time when a very thoroughly cooked crayfish was found in the bottom of the big picnic coffee pot as the last cup had been poured and enjoyed. (We remember this incident probably because we were one of the children who used the coffee pot on a crayfish-hunting expedition and failed to empty the pot thoroughly before returning it to the cook.) We still remember the chocolate cake which proved to be as delectable to the little red ants as it did to the picnickers who wonder to this day whether the ants moved in before or after much of the cake had been eaten.

We may say in looking back that life was simpler then and we required less to make us happy. There were fewer inventions which had moved into our lives to become necessary luxuries. Yet we cannot use the complexities of life today as an excuse for our lack of appreciation of the simple life now, for every generation could use the same false reasoning. The basic ingredients for the good family life have not changed over the years.

If we would carry the lessons learned from our own happy childhood memories to this generation and would pass on the formula for the good life, we would put love, respect for each other, fun moments shared together, happy hours of companionship above the mad scramble for material possessions. We would hesitate before sacrificing time with our families to earn more money to buy more possessions. Rather we would make *time* to spend with our families. We would recognize that it is not so much how much *money* we spend on our children but how much *time* we spend with them that is important. Nothing we can buy can substitute for the gift of ourselves.

We would remember the words of the Sermon on the Mount, which admonishes us: "Lay not up for yourselves treasures upon earth where moth and rust doth corrupt . . . for where your treasure is there your heart be also." For to our families, what we give from the heart is of more significance than that which we give from treasure troves. The love we earn in return surpasses in value anything that can be bought.

Family Fun and Activities

I

The Need to Play

From earliest time man has created. In this respect he has differed from the animals. Animals built their nests, tunneled out their homes, sought out their lairs; built with wood or fashioned with wax or mud. Whatever the materials used, wherever their homes, however they made them, they did so by instinct, driven by their struggle for survival. Each species developed its own peculiar type of home suited to its needs. Thus an anthill is recognizable as an anthill in whatever part of the world it is found, whatever the species or variety that built it. A honeycomb looks much the same wherever you find it in the world. An oriole's nest can never be mistaken for that of a robin although both belong to the same order of perching birds, the passerines. The song of a warbler is much the same as it was generations ago.

Man also was driven by the instinct for survival. He fashioned shelters, clothing, weapons and tools. But while animals followed the same patterns generation after generation, aeon after aeon, man did not. He improved upon his inventions. He did more than that; he embellished them. For man it was not enough that his shelter, his tools, his clothing and even his weapons be functional; they must also be beautiful. With man, the urge to create was as strong as the instinct for survival. And here comes to light another difference between man and animal which for want of a better term we call the evidence of soul. When man produces from necessity he is meeting the challenge for survival; when he produces for the sake of beauty, he is creating. The first is a product of the mind, the latter a product of the soul. The first produces the materials for existence; the latter creates beauty.

I

The drive to create has not only widened the difference between man and animal; it has created differences in the life habits of man himself. Consider man in various parts of the world. Each has gone about filling his needs in the ways most suited to his environment. Each has developed his own type of shelter, tools, clothing, weapons and religion. He has developed a form of family and community life and lives under some kind of organized government. But whether he lives in the Arctic or the South Seas, in a stone chalet or an adobe; whether he be black, yellow, brown or white; a South American gaucho or a Swiss mountain climber; whatever his religion is—Mohammedan, Buddhist or Christian; whether he be a member of the most primitive tribe or citizen in a highly civilized or complex society, he has not spent all his time in his struggle for existence. He has found the time or made the time for play. From this play has emerged music, literature, the drama, the dance, the constructive and manual arts, the fine arts, games and contests, experiments in human relations and the ever-widening knowledge about his world and the universe of which it is a part.

Man is his noblest self when he is engaged in creative play. In the act of creation, man emulates his Creator and fans the spark of divinity within him until it glows. Creative play might be described as man's search for God. In creating man must give his whole self to the act; he must give his best self. There is no room for impatience, pettiness, anger, evil passion or hatred, for the mind is a strict taskmaster and will not tolerate such obstacles to the even flow of thought that is necessary in the act of creating. When the flow is interrupted, the product falls far short of the mark of perfection the mind demands. To bring complete satisfaction, the artist must achieve the level of perfection he has set for himself whether he is composing a sonata, writing a poem, trying to develop a new variety of rose or attempting to set a new world's record for the high hurdles. The mind in creative play is focused upon the task at hand. If it is concerned with the thoughts of personal recognition, public acclaim or the financial gain the end product may bring, the results are inferior. These may be the secondary benefits, but they can never be the motivating factors; real creativity springs from inspiration not bribery. Real creativity and true play are motivated by a deep personal need for release from tensions, an urgent need for self-expression or a desperate need for relaxation.

Wherever man lives, whatever his mode of life, the basic need for play is the same. Whether he be African bushman or a sophisticated New Yorker, consciously or unconsciously he feels the need for play and invests some of his time in the serious pursuit of it. And he who does make a wise investment, for psychiatrists have found that good mental health is directly related to the capacity and willingness of individuals to play.

While the need to play is inherent, the most constructive and satisfying play is learned. The ability to play is not accidentally endowed nor is it an inherited trait. Personality traits and psychological needs may provide a basis for interest in one form of recreation or another, but an individual must be encouraged and, in most cases, instructed so that he may derive the full measure of satisfaction from his endeavors.

The ability to play is a learned ability. Children must be given ample opportunity to play alone and with their families and others, at home or elsewhere. The provision of play opportunities is the function first of the home and then of the school, the church and the government. Parents who know how to play creatively and have avocational interests are more likely to stimulate the development of similar interests in their children. They not only stimulate their children by example but each benefits from the stimulating and satisfying sharing of family interests. In happy home situations where good morale exists, the best preventive program against the insidious disease of delinquency is built up. Delinquency is a symptom of social maladjustment and of poor morale rather than poor morals.

Working man in the Western world has more leisure than ever before in history. His life span is longer and his work span shorter than ever before. The ability to play becomes vitally important under these conditions. The child who knows how to play becomes the adult who plays. He moves into old age more calmly and more confidently than the untrained. He keeps his interests alive until the very end, living fully all the days of his life in contrast to those who sit empty-handed, empty-minded, filled with a loneliness they have no means to combat.

Creative play is, then, not a sin nor a luxury as some would have us believe. Neither is it a part of childhood to be put aside with other childish things. It is rather a companion and helpmate of work. It is as necessary a part of everyday living as food. Where food nourishes the body, play nourishes the mind. Play dispels the fatigues that build up in a workday. It banishes the boredom which has settled upon us after hours of monotonous, repetitious labor. It stimulates the mind and increases one's capacity for enjoying life. The individual who is attuned to the miracles of life that surround him in the wonders of nature, who knows the comfort and stimulation of companions and friends, who is stimulated by the beauties of sound, color and rhythmic motion is a happier and healthier person.

It cannot be denied that there is a direct relationship between the emotions and physical health. Boredom contributes to mental and physical deterioration as geriatricians have discovered. No person who has learned and developed the ability to play creatively is ever bored. Through his play he is constantly challenged to find answers to questions he meets at every turn. He is driven by a force from within that challenges him to learn more, to do something better than he did it the last time, to make something that is beautiful or functional or to seek out some rare stamp or coin to augment his collection.

All of us have this inner drive to create, but not all have learned the ways of satisfying its demands. Those who have are happy, healthy, emotionally mature and secure people. Those who have not learned the magic formula wear their lives away dissatisfied and discontented, never realizing their full potentialities, never understanding their unhappiness, being aware of it but ignorant of the means to dispel it.

The more complex our lives become, the higher our civilization, the more numerous our inventions, the more we complicate our lives with labor-saving devices, the greater the need for play in our lives. Everything that makes our lives easier, every piece of equipment that takes the work out of labor contributes to our physical comfort but robs us of a sense of achievement that results from a challenge that has been successfully met. The satisfactions that stem from the fulfillment of man's need to create are easily lost in a mechanized civilization. Man, more than ever in his social history, needs a design for creative living. He needs to know how to play. He must be prepared to meet the challenge of leisure. The earliest training must begin in the home.

2

Play Begins at Home

A child's earliest training normally begins in the home. Play, an integral part of his training, must have its beginnings there. For the ability to play like the ability to talk is a learned one and the child must be trained and encouraged in the development of this as in any other ability.

Talents and aptitudes are inherited. We say a child is a "born musician," a "born mimic," or a "born leader." We recognize that some children have inherited traits that develop rapidly in response to stimulation and training in those areas. A child born into a musical family probably inherits musical talent and because of the family interest in music rapidly develops his musical ability to its full capacity. Here then is the ideal combination, the marriage between inherent traits and environmental influences.

The real tragedy occurs when a child with a particular talent is born into a family which does nothing to develop it, and his environment outside the family offers no opportunity to exploit his talent. When such a potential resource is allowed to remain undeveloped, it is as if it never existed. Unless a talent is utilized within the lifetime of its possessor, it can never become a reality.

The talents and potentialities of its citizens are as valuable a resource to a country as the coal, oil or minerals which lie buried beneath the soil within its boundaries. There is one important difference, however. The natural resources undiscovered in one era can be uncovered in another to benefit generations for years to come. Human resources, measurable only in terms of talents which have been cultivated and aptitudes which have been exploited to the full, unless utilized within the lifetime of the possessor, are irretrievably lost.

We will never know how many times a brilliant mind which might have produced a means of alleviating the sufferings of untold thousands has been crushed under the weight of its indifferent environment so that it never came to fulfillment. For every Beethoven or Bach, who knows how many musical geniuses have died without having written a note because the soil in which they grew was barren of the opportunities which nurture such talent? For every Rembrandt and Gainsborough there have probably been thousands of talented individuals who through their own weaknesses or under the pressures of their environment (which more often measures success by the size of the bank account than by the quality of work on a canvas) have abandoned their talents for more certain and lucrative pursuits. In such instances the individual, however, has had the power to make a choice. He knew his talent and chose the way in which he would use it. The choice, whether good or bad, gives evidence that opportunity for the recognition and development of his potentialities has at least been offered.

Any individual, if he is to make his mark at all, must have chances to develop his native abilities. Play is one of the strongest factors in the discovery of such talents. Many interests and talents come to light during play activities. The alert and interested parent fosters and encourages these interests.

Many an adult who has been able to carry over his most stimulating interest into his work can trace the beginnings of this happy combination to his early training. When the talent is not sufficiently great to sustain the person financially he may seek work in other fields but still foster his interests and enjoy them as avocations throughout his life. Either individual is fortunate for he has found the things which enrich his life and give it meaning which it might not otherwise have had.

Foundations for the good life are laid in the home. Good physical health has its beginnings there. Good mental health begins there. We know more about giving the child a good start in his physical life than we do about helping him to a good start in his emotional life. We recognize the importance of proper diet, sufficient rest and relaxation, exercise, shots and vaccinations in the maintenance of physical health. We know less about the ways to develop sound emotional health and the factors therein involved. We understand headaches, stomach-aches, sniffles, elevated temperatures, sore throats and pains as symptoms of physical ill-health. We are less prone to recognize unhappiness, moody spells, overdependence and irritability as symptoms of poor mental health.

To achieve and maintain mental health for ourselves and our children we must have an understanding of our personalities and some effective methods of first aid for emotional ills. We must know something about our instinctive drives, both constructive and destructive, and how the mismanagement of these drives is related to poor mental health. Good recreational activities provide socially acceptable outlets for the instinctive aggressive drive. Sports and competitive games of active or sedentary type serve as good safety valves for this drive. Another psychological instinct—the erotic, constructive or creative drive —finds fulfillment in the producing of something—a poem, a song, a wood carving, a ceramic piece or even a pie. Less satisfying are those activities in which we have only a passive interest such as entertainments: the concerts, the theater arts, the athletic contests at which we are spectators. They afford us opportunities for relaxation through vicarious participation only.

Play satisfies a deep-seated psychological need. Mentally healthy people supplement their daily work with this medium. Even those with little leisure make time for it. The choice of activity is modified by their experiences and mode of living. Early childhood training, too, has bearing not only on the ability to play but the areas in which an adult finds expression. This early training becomes more vital as the need for recreative play increases since people now have more leisure than they did generations ago. Their jobs, however, afford them little opportunity for pioneering, for creative endeavor or for expressing their aggressive needs.

At a study made at the Menninger Clinic in Kansas, concrete relationships between avocations and mental health were revealed. The hobbies of a well-adjusted group were compared both in number and duration with those of psychiatric patients. The hobbies of the well-adjusted group were far in excess both in number and intensity to those of the patients. While this does not prove that a hobby keeps a person mentally well, it can be interpreted as meaning that a well-adjusted person learns how to play and includes play as an important part of his life more frequently than the maladjusted person does. There is considerable scientific evidence that the healthy personality not only plays but takes his play seriously. There is also evidence that the inability and unwillingness to play is evidence of insecurity and a disordered aspect of personality.

An awareness of these facts and an acceptance of the importance of early training throws the responsibilty for giving a child a good start in physical and emotional health directly into the laps of the parents and the home. But even a good home is limited in the amount and extent of opportunities in creative play it can afford the child. The school, the church and the community have their responsibilities, too. The school through its curriculum, facilities and quality of its teachers; the church in its scope of guidance and capabilities of leadership; the community in its long-range view, understanding and acceptance of the responsibility for the provision of sufficient recreation areas and facilities adequately equipped and manned with well-trained leadership all play an important part. Yet behind these institutions are the citizenry, the parents, the businessmen and civic leaders, the teachers and the clergy whose understanding and acceptance of their community responsibilities are directly related to the quantity and quality of community life.

A good home with interested parents gives a child his start in creative living. The community supplements this beginning and fosters its growth through the provision of leadership and facilities far beyond the scope of the normal home. There is no substitute for group experience. There is no substitute for parental love or the experience of being loved and the act of returning love so necessary in the establishment of a feeling of security in a child. There is real security in a family that plays together. The lessons in self-discipline, respect for other people's rights and property, self-control, the business of give and take, the acceptance of and respect for rules and laws are learned in the home in family play as well as in the school and on the playground. A child needs the opportunity of belonging to several groups —in his school, in his church, on his playground. The ability to identify oneself with a group and to get along with people is part of good mental health. The psychiatric patient during his illness is incapable of feeling comfortable with other people and finds it difficult to identify with or belong to a social unit.

Parents who want their children to grow in mental as well as in physical stature and eventually to achieve maturity will begin their child's training in the home and strive to have it continued in the community. They will recognize the importance of creative leisure in this early training program. They will understand its importance in their own lives.

3

A Balanced Leisure Time Diet

Balance is always a valuable component of any program. Mother Nature herself is always engaged in a struggle to maintain a proper balance and when that balance is disturbed, disaster results. Man as a child of Nature must regulate his life and keep all the elements in balance, or disaster, in one form or another, is his fate. It was no dull-witted, inexperienced fool who first made the statement, "All work and no play makes Jack a dull boy." But even in his play Jack must maintain a balance to assure a sturdy and vigorous growth, mentally, socially, physically and spiritually. It is only when these elements of growth are kept in balance that maturity is achieved. Man has added much to his knowledge pertaining to the importance of balanced diet to his health. No one would argue the point that to derive the full benefits from our food we must participate in the business of eating. To sit at a laden table and watch others eat while we sit idly by neither satisfies our physical hunger nor does it nourish us. Yet in our leisure time, we delude ourselves into thinking that by watching others at play whether on the ball field, in the concert hall or on the stage, we can find nourishment and satisfaction for our needs. It is true that there is a place in our lives for passive forms of recreation since many of us never achieve the top level of performance in any one skill. We make up the audience who view with appreciation the expert performers. To perform and to appreciate are important parts of living but they too must be kept in a balance. For most of us our appreciation level is higher than our performance level, but the better our own performance, the greater our ability to appreciate. The amateur musician who has struggled with scales and chords has more respect for the perfection of the artist-performer than one who has not. The dub golfer appreciates the smooth performance of the expert more than does the uninitiated.

When we think in terms of a balanced leisure time program, we must allow some time for passive recreation but our major emphasis must be on the participation level where we actually engage in the act of creating. While we may have talents in certain areas, the abilities to create must be taught and encouraged—more, they must be steadily impelled.

No civilization can long remain in a position of leadership if its citizens are content to adopt the products of the creative powers of others and are willing to let their own wither and die of disuse. Americans have built their greatness with their inventive genius and their creative powers. To keep America great we must keep alive the abilities that made her so. We have invented or developed media whereby the creative efforts of a few can be put to the passive recreational use of millions. This can have advantages for the few performers who can reap large financial benefits because of this wide coverage but it tends to destroy the creative ability of those who submit to this form of passive entertainment. We are rapidly becoming a nation of button-pushers, platter-spinners, television-viewers, sports fans, moviegoers and knob-twirlers. We no longer make most of the things we need. We no longer do things. We have become a buying public and a watching public. We have taken the record player, the radio and the television set in exchange for the piano, the game room and the library. In the effort to find enjoyment we have pursued pleasure to a point of surfeit and have deadened our abilities to enjoy. We have become bystanders at the curb who watch the parade of life pass by and wonder why we feel so out of things. Our enjoyment of life is commensurate with our ability to live. To live we must create. Life without creating is no life at all but a dull, monotonous counting off of the days.

In considering the participation program, we must maintain balance thereby introducing the possibilities of creative endeavor in several areas, striving to develop a personality that is many-sided, knowing that each facet brings new beauty, new joy and richness to our lives. In our food diets we are becoming increasingly aware of the importance of the various vitamins and minerals and of the life-giving qualities of the proteins and the carbohydrates. The vitamins are not new substances, they were there all the time. It is only our realizations of their importance that is new. So it is with the components of a good leisure time diet. The elements are not new. They are as old as the history of man. It is our growing realization of their importance in man's life that is new. In the good recreation diet there are nine vital areas of creative endeavor. Like the vitamins they are rarely found alone but in combination with others. They are equally important. One cannot substitute effectively for another. We need them all. Each fills a particular need. Each supplies some needed nourishment. Unless we employ them, all we never quite satisfy all our needs. We never become completely whole.

The nine areas of creative endeavor which will be discussed in ensuing chapters as vital components of family play are:

1. Social activities
2. Musical activities
3. Rhythmic activities
4. Linguistic activities
5. Nature activities
6. Service activities
7. Constructive activities or arts and crafts
8. Physical activities
9. Dramatic activities

Family Check List

A family will find it interesting to check its list of family play activities against the list of nine types to see how complete its list is.

THE LIST OF NINE TYPES OF RECREATIONAL ACTIVITIES
WITH EXAMPLES OF EACH

1. Social activities
   Playing cards and other games—Family parties, picnics, reunions —Attending church socials or other parties as a family unit
2. Musical activities
   Sing sessions, family orchestra—Attending concerts—Belonging

to orchestra or chorus—Taking music lessons
3. Rhythmic activities
    *Taking dancing lessons—Attending dance concerts or the ballet
    —Going to social or square dances—Family rhythm band—
    Playing rhythmic games*
4. Linguistic activities
    *Reading aloud to each other—Discussions on current events—
    Reciting poetry and nursery rhymes—Just talking—Reading for
    fun as well as with a serious purpose*
5. Nature activities
    *Going on nature hikes—Studying the stars—Learning to predict
    weather—Feeding the birds in winter and learning to recognize
    the various species—Putting up birdhouses and studying the
    habits of the birds—Learning about growing things with house
    plants, in a garden or terrarium—Raising fish in a home aquar-
    ium—Having a dog, cat or other pets—Studying the trees, wild
    flowers, rocks*
6. Service activities
    *Belonging to service organizations which do things for others
    (Camp Fire, Girl and Boy Scouts, church service committees)—
    Helping with campaigns and fund-raising projects—Just being
    neighborly*
7. Constructive activities (arts and crafts)
    *Making things together in wood shop, at the sewing table—
    Painting, enameling, clay modeling—Developing and printing
    pictures—Cooking for the fun of it as well as for necessity*
8. Physical activities
    *Ping-pong, croquet, badminton, horseshoes and other back yard
    games—Playing catch with a baseball—Baseball, golf, bowling,
    tennis—Swimming and boating—Hiking—Roller and ice skating*
9. Dramatic activities
    *Dramatic games (charades, pantomimes)—Participating in
    amateur dramatic productions at church, school, community
    center or theater—Belonging to play-reading groups—Attend-
    ing plays*

These are only a few of dozens of possibilities in each category. Add the other activities you like that are not listed here. If you have checked at least one activity in each group you have the beginnings of a well-rounded recreational program. If you find several checks in some types and none in others, your recreation diet is not exactly well balanced.

4

Family Fun with Arts and Crafts

No one can have too many friends. No one can have too many skills. Skills like friends help to fill many hours with joy. They are a comfort in times of sorrow and distress.

Our hands which are wonderfully manipulative tools can, when trained, produce objects both useful and beautiful. The media of creation in the fields of arts and crafts are almost unlimited. Wood, stone, shells, leather, metals, yarns, clay, paints, fabrics and natural materials offer endless possibilities for experimentation in this field. Creative play in arts and crafts is both a satisfying and practical form of play. Articles can be made for use in the home, for gifts and for sale. Those sold can help to finance further experimentation and can supplement pensions, as our older retired craftsmen have discovered.

As healthful living develops a resistance against disease so, at the workbench or easel, protective armor is developed against the stresses, strains and tensions of modern living. Each article fashioned painstakingly by hand is not only a tribute to the skill and creativity of its maker, it is concrete evidence of a challenge met and taken up. The battle cry of the do-it-yourself craftsman is: "Anyone can buy one ready-made. I made this myself!"

Every time a craftsman completes a project he gains in self-confidence and develops a spirit of independence which carries over into other endeavors. Each experience with tools and raw materials is a challenge—a venture into the unknown. Each article completed is a personal triumph in perseverance and skill for the creator.

Like the mother crow in Aesop's fable who thought her baby the most beautiful of all, so the things we make ourselves have merit in our eyes. This is one of the phenomena of the game. Two people of different levels of skills working side by side can get the same amount of personal satisfaction from their finished products. The fact that an

article produced by the one is superior to that produced by the other in no way deprives the maker of the inferior one of intense satisfaction. Each has his own goals, each sets his own level of achievement. If he reaches that goal he is satisfied. This is one of the reasons why arts and crafts are such good family activities. The child does not expect to surpass the quality of the article made by the parent (though he sometimes does) and so is not discouraged by the results. Thus parents and child may work at the same bench or work table enjoying close companionship which often develops under such situations. Each works at his own level, neither having to step down to the level of the other. Each enjoys his own satisfactions. Each can praise the achievement of the other with sincere enthusiasm. They are not in competition with each other, only with themselves in their efforts to improve their skills.

There is no final end in arts and crafts except that caused by a cessation of interest. No matter what level of achievement a craftsman reaches, there is always another higher one. At work on one piece the craftsman's mind is already planning and creating the next. This may account for the fact that failures are not fatally discouraging. The future always holds hopes. The craftsman making a mistake which may ruin one piece consoles himself that he has learned a valuable lesson which will prevent him from making that error again.

Interests in arts and crafts most often have their beginnings in the home. Talents, aptitudes and abilities like any living things must be given the nourishment of encouragement before they can flourish and bloom. A home where tools, workbenches and opportunities for experimentation in all manner of arts and crafts are provided is a good home. A child who never has the opportunity to develop manual dexterity and use it in enjoyable activities is deprived of one of the most satisfying means of self-expression. More, he is much too dependent upon machines. Let his machines break down and he is reduced to a state of helplessness. He knows only how to function as a man with a machine, not as a man alone. The individuals who boast: "I can't cook. I can't even boil water without burning it! I wouldn't know how to sew a button on. I don't know one end of a hammer from another," are not only fools to be pitied but are a disgrace to the human race. Not only have they been allowed to squander their inheritance but they even brag about the waste.

Whether a family lives in an apartment or house, there are many types of arts and crafts which can be promoted in either type of dwelling. Suggestions for several types follow. Some directions for some one-shot projects for special occasions are also given in detail.

ONE-SHOT CRAFT PROJECTS FOR SPECIAL OCCASIONS

Christmas Candles (Block Paraffin Style)

Attractive candles can be made by several methods. One of the simplest is the method which uses blocks of paraffin. The thing to remember in working with paraffin is that it is highly inflammable and extreme care should be used when heating it. Heat it over a low fire slowly in a pan that is large enough so that the quantity being heated never comes beyond the center mark of the pan. To make block candles proceed in this manner:

1. First cover all working surfaces, table and floor with several layers of newspapers. (Wax is difficult to remove from furniture and floors!)

2. Heat an old cake tin or cookie sheet over a low flame.

3. Now rub the largest surface of one side of each of two blocks against the pan until the wax begins to melt. Put the two melted surfaces together and hold in place until the wax cools and the two blocks are fused together. Now take a length of string for a wick and lay it along the center of the two fused blocks lengthwise. See upper left sketch. Now take two more blocks and fuse them together. Take these two blocks and rub one side of one block on the warm surface of the pan and fuse the two blocks to the first two blocks being careful to keep the wick in its proper position. Lower left sketch.

4. Melt several blocks cautiously in a pan over a low flame. When

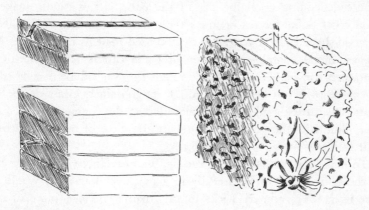

all are melted remove from stove, place on a surface well protected with newspapers. Beat melted wax with a fork or egg beater until the wax is frothy. Spread the frothy mixture over all the surfaces except the top of the block candle you have just made, patting it on with a fork.

5. Before the froth is completely cooled and hardened, sprinkle with glitter, decorate it with sequins holding them in place with straight pins, or stick bits of Christmas greenery into the wax. See sketch on right. Anchor the candle with melted wax in a small aluminum dish or on an attractive saucer.

This is a project which all the family can participate in. The candles can be made for home consumption or as gifts to friends. When lighted they burn with an inner glow that is quite beautiful. Because they are so large they will burn many, many hours and can be saved from one year to the next.

Christmas Candles (Melted Style)

When paraffin is melted and poured into containers which are prepared beforehand with wicks, possibilities are as innumerable as the shapes of containers you have. Frozen fruit juice cans which are small cylinders make good Christmas candles. Bread pans will make unusual candles. As many as three wicks can be arranged in one such candle depending upon the size of the pan. Such a candle makes a good focal point for a Christmas table decoration. Gelatin molds or any odd-shaped metal container can be used for this type candle. We suggest metal containers because after the candle is completed the containers can be heated enough to melt the wax of the outside edges of candle so it can be slipped out of its container. Glass or ceramic containers can be used and the candle left in the container. This, however, eliminates the possibility of seeing the glow of the whole candle as it burns.

To make the melted type of candle, use paraffin or old candle ends of the same color. Melt carefully in a pan over low heat. While the wax is melting, prepare wicks in this manner: Tie a piece of cord around a stick long enough to reach across the top of the container to be used. Leave one end of the knotted string long enough to reach down to the bottom of the container. If the cord is pulled through melted wax and run through your fingers it will become stiff and will stay straight until the wax is poured into the container.

When the wax in the pan is melted, pour it carefully into the container which has been prepared with the wick on a stick. When the wax is cooled and hard, heat the outside surfaces of the container carefully over a low flame and pull the finished candle out by the stick. Cut off the stick and your candle is finished.

This type of candle can be treated with whipped frothy wax in the same manner described in block-paraffin-style candles.

If you use gelatin molds for candle molds, make some candles which fill the mold and some which are no more than a half-inch thick. These can be floated in a large flower bowl and lighted for an unusual effect.

Christmas Wreaths

Use branches you have cut from your Christmas tree or greens you have purchased for this purpose. Bend the branch into a circle formation and fasten ends with green-covered or red-covered bell wire. Spray lightly hit-and-miss style with silver or white paint which comes in spray cans. Decorate with a bow of red plastic and colored Christmas tree bells or various-sized bells tied to red streamers of varying lengths of one-inch ribbon.

Christmas Sprays

Take branches of fir or balsam trees. Spray lightly here and there with white or silver paint. Decorate with a large bow of red plastic ribbon. Tie silver bells here and there in the smaller branches or suspend them on the ends of one-inch red ribbon of varying lengths and tie under the bow so that the bells extend below it.

May Baskets

Surprise your friends by leaving May baskets at their doors where they will find them with the morning paper on the first day of May. Decorate bread pans, berry baskets or cardboard boxes with paint, crepe paper or tissue paper and ribbons. Tin containers need not be lined but cardboard or baskets should be lined with aluminum foil. Fill with soil, growing plants (wild flowers if possible) and moss.

This is a project which the whole family can participate in.

Easter Baskets

Easter baskets filled and decorated in professional style are enjoyed not only by the recipients but by the persons who have all the fun of assembling the contents and arranging them.

You will need baskets, colored grass, jelly beans, a variety of candy eggs, dyed hard-cooked eggs, Easter cards and any other surprises you might wish to enclose. Crayons, coloring books, books, a small doll, pocket knife or some other treasure dear to the heart of a child will be welcome additions.

Fill the container about three-quarters full with grass, arrange the candy, eggs and other treasures in the basket. Cover the whole basket with a sheet of colored cellophane paper. Gather the paper together at the top and tie with a piece of ribbon. Staple the Easter card to this portion of the cellophane.

If you have several children to make baskets for in your own family and your children wish to give them as gifts to their friends, you will find it not only cheaper to make your own but a lot of fun. Baskets need not be big to be attractive. Sometimes the smallest ones are the most beautiful.

No one ever grows too old to enjoy Easter baskets. They can be prepared for every member of the family from grandmother down to the baby. Grandmother's may be small but contain a new pair of earrings or some other piece of jewelry. Dad's Easter eggs may be golf balls.

The preparation of the baskets can be as secretive a process as that of wrapping Christmas presents. If a table with the makings is set up in a room which can be closed off, each member can then arrange for time in the room to fix his own baskets for other members of the family. The surprise gift can be wrapped beyond recognition before being placed in the basket so that its identity is not known until the basket is opened on Easter morning. When baskets are being prepared for friends, the whole family can gather around the table and work together. A production line can be set up so that each member of the family makes his contribution. The youngest can put in the grass and the jelly beans, the next member arranges some of the other contents, the most artistic member of the family puts on the final touches and arranges and staples the cellophane into place.

The Easter egg coloring process which is another operation that all members can participate in is done a day or so before the baskets are to be filled so that the eggs are in readiness. With the eggs as with the baskets, each makes his own special contribution. Those who are good with pen and ink can make drawings on the eggs. Those good at making hats or other decorations can make "egg heads." Sequins, beads, rhinestones and other such materials can be used to decorate eggs so that they are works of art. Those adept with paints can decorate the eggs with landscapes, seascapes, pictures of birds or butterflies. In some families, the decorating of the eggs is a cherished Easter tradition. The eggs are lavishly decorated. Friends receiving the eggs value them highly and save them from year to year for decorations or for the Easter table centerpiece.

Christmas Stockings

Christmas stockings made of red oilcloth or felt decorated in tasteful designs and sometimes inscribed with the owner's name can be made as gifts to friends as well as for home use at the family fireplace. The older, more skilled members of the family do the more complicated processes and the younger children help in those which they can perform well.

Cut a pattern from heavy wrapping paper. Make patterns of different sizes. Pin to double thickness of the material to be used and cut around the outline with pinking shears. Sew the two pieces together on the sewing machine. If names are to be sewed on, this must be done before the two pieces are sewed together. Letters can be cut from white material of the same variety as that used for the stockings. If oilcloth is used, the letters can be cemented onto the stocking with a plastic cement. If felt is used, the names can be embroidered on with a running or cross stitch or they can be cut from white felt and sewed on by hand or by machine. The important thing is that the more members of the family who participate, the better the results. The warm family feeling which is created is as beautiful as the articles produced.

Halloween Jack-o'-lanterns

The fashioning of Halloween jack-o'-lanterns is a wonderful family fun project. Two kinds are possible. One method uses the cutting of a saucer-shaped piece from the top of the pumpkin. The insides are then scooped out. A face is then cut on one side of the pumpkin. A candle or electric light is inserted into the pumpkin so that it can be lighted from within. Another method does not involve cutting. A pumpkin or Hubbard squash is used as the head. The features of the face are made from other vegetables. The nose may be a piece of the carrot, a half red pepper or a half potato. Eyes may be prunes, figs, parts of apples or whatever. Ears are half green peppers. The family can have fun trying various pieces of vegetables and fruits to see which gives the best effect.

Some families make a tradition of decorating their front porches or yards with Halloween decorations. Old jeans and a sweat shirt stuffed and tied together with a belt make a grotesque body for an equally grotesque head fashioned of a squash or pumpkin. Sometimes these bodies are arranged in lifelike poses in lawn furniture. One family constructed a sawhorse mount with a pumpkin head for the pumpkin-headed dummy. Families who make a practice of concocting weird Halloween decorations spend hours figuring new and different ones each year. This involves family conferences which add to the fun.

Outdoor Christmas Decorations

It is always fun to drive down residential streets during the Yuletide season where families have gone to great lengths to decorate the outsides of their houses and their lawns with simple or elaborate Christmas decorations.

Such decorations can be bought but many are made from original or commercial patterns in the family workshops. Needless to say, many happy hours have been spent in the preparation. As with other family craft projects, some part of the job should be assigned to every interested family member. Even the youngest can contribute. Hand sanding, painting on the first undercoat, helping to arrange and erect the various parts of a Christmas manger or Santa and his reindeer scene can keep every member of the family busy.

Christmas Tree Decorations

The most-loved decorations on the tree are often primitive ones constructed by the younger members in the family from paper, popcorn, cranberries, colored foil or wood.

Bells, gingerbread boys, stars, Christmas trees, boots and other appropriate shapes can be cut from wood on the jig saw or with a coping saw and painted and decorated in bright colors. They can be brightened and enhanced by working a design with a colorless cement and then sprinkled with glitter or sequins. The decorating process can be a family project. The kitchen or dining room table well protected with newspapers can be the center of operation. All the makings for the decorations can be assembled here. With all the wood articles cut out and painted and ready to decorate, the family goes to work dressing them up. Everyone gets in the act. *And* everyone helps to clean up later! When Christmas comes and friends drop in to see your tree, guess which decorations will get the most attention!

DO-IT-YOURSELF PROJECTS

Tools for crafts are as important household items as radio, television set, piano. Families who live in apartments must limit themselves in the types of equipment they have space for, but even small quarters do not keep the amateur craftsman from enjoying his favorite craft avocation.

Do-it-yourself kits have made many projects possible for the apartment dweller. With all the work which requires the power tools prepared in the factory or shop, the purchaser needs only work space in which to do the assembling and finishing. Woodworking projects from small shelves to larger pieces such as tables, Dutch cupboards or cabinets are prepared in kits. The hobbyist can then assemble and finish with loving care a piece of furniture for his home.

Many times the prepared kit fits into other family interests. For example, it is possible to buy high-fidelity radio and phonograph kits. One can assemble his own tape recording outfit or make his own electronic flash kit for use with a camera. Camping families can build their own boats from kits. Long winter evenings become something to look forward to when such projects are on the agenda.

Winter is the time to get other camping equipment mended or made. This is the time rope lengths for rigging the tents and the tarpaulin are prepared and the rope ends served. The carry-all to fit on the top of the car is constructed at this time for the long-planned summer camping trip months before it will be used.

Dark rooms have been built in apartment closets and work as well as more spacious ones built in basements. Small electric kilns for enameling on metal which operate on 110-volt lines are now available. Amateur painters can paint in water colors or oils. They can paint on paper, canvas, metal wastebaskets, trays, salad bowls. Pennsylvania Dutch designs are applied by one method or another to new pieces of furniture or pieces found in an antique shop or in a farmer's barn and gleefully brought home to be refinished and decorated.

Home owners readily succumb to the opportunities to finish off portions of the attic space or basement to make the extra bedroom or rumpus room. The do-it-yourself industry is booming. Everyone can get into this wonderful act.

Many of the projects are ones which can involve many members of the family. The more persons involved, the more meaning the project takes on. Family pride in a project jointly accomplished is a joy to see.

Whatever the interest, there is a project to satisfy the craftsman of any age with any amount of home work space. Visit hobby houses, lumberyards, home show displays, camera or craft shops. Listen to the conversations that go on among hobbyists and between salesmen and hobbyists. The air is electric with enthusiastic talk and original ideas. Watch the faces of these people. There is no boredom reflected there, only interest and eager anticipation.

THE FAMILY CRAFT PROGRAM

There are a number of crafts which family members from five years on up will find satisfying. Articles for self-use or for gifts can be made for less than it is possible to purchase machine-made ones and for much less than hand-made articles of similar quality would cost. A number of these media are discussed in the following paragraphs.

Leather Craft

For those who do not wish to purchase kits of tools, precut, prepunched leather projects are available from craft houses. Projects include coin purses, key cases, billfolds, moccasins, belts, wallets of every variety of leather, shape and color. These, however, are more expensive than those made when the craftsman cuts his own projects, shapes and punches as well as laces them. They provide the fun of assembling but none of the pleasure which comes from the business of starting from scratch and doing one's own cutting, tooling, punching and lacing.

The true craftsman scorns the precut, prepunched deal and prefers to start at the beginning. If the family plans to do a large volume of work and wants to do its own designing, this is not only the more fun way but the more economical. Leather is then purchased by the whole, half or quarter hide. Lacing, snaps, rivets, eyelets and other necessary findings can be purchased in volume at a saving.

If a family is just beginning in leatherwork, it is wise to work with project kits first. If one member can enroll in a leather craft course to learn the tricks of the trade, the whole family can benefit. A minimum list of tools necessary for leathercraft is given here. Where several persons will be working at the same time you will need more of some of the tools so more than one can work at the same process simultaneously. These will be so designated on the list by asterisks. Lists are given for both leather tooling and leather carving and stamping. Patterns, designs and directions for making are readily available at your hobby craft shop. Scrap leather suitable for small projects can be purchased at the upholsterer's or at the craft house by the pound.

MINIMUM LEATHER TOOLING TOOL LIST

1. Metal square or ruler
2. All-purpose belt punch
3. Punch with interchangeable punches
4. Single-edge razor blades for cutting*
5. Leather modeling tools*
6. Snap and eyelet setter kit
7. Scratch awl*
8. Pieces of marble, Masonite or slate*
9. Wooden mallet
10. Lacing needles*

With this set you can make purses and handbags, billfolds, key cases, notebooks, wallets, coin purses, brief cases, leather-covered tooled table tops, wastebackets, gloves, moccasins, leather vests, etc.

LEATHER FINDINGS AND SUPPLIES

Beside the leather and tools you will need the following minimum list of items:

1. Snaps
2. Rivets
3. Eyelets
4. Key chains
5. Leather cement (rubber base)
6. Findings for leather purses would include catches, strap hangers and belt buckles

7. Celluloid in sheets for use in identification cases, etc.
8. Lacing (leather or plastic)
9. Linen waxed sewing thread

LEATHER CARVING

A leather carving kit involves all the tools needed for tooling plus these items:

1. Carving knife with interchangeable blades
2. Minimum list of dies:
   a. Plain and checked bevelers of two sizes
   b. Pear shaders, both plain and checked
   c. Mule-foot tools of two sizes
   d. Seeders of two sizes
   e. Three or four background tools of different designs
   f. Veiner

With this list a good variety of effects can be achieved. Commercial designs suggesting ways of executing them and the tools needed can be purchased at your hobby store. You can work out details of designs in any way you wish. Alphabets which enable you to monogram or even work a whole name into your design are also available. If you are sufficiently artistic to work out your own designs so much the better, but craftsmen who cannot need not be handicapped by this limitation. A purse well executed from a commercial design is beautiful and gives the craftsman all the fun of working the design and assembling and lacing the project. When you have finished such a project, the fact that you used a commercial design will not take away from satisfaction.

Types of Leathercraft

Before you buy any kit of tools, it is wise to know which type of leatherwork you want to do. A brief description of each type is given here.

LEATHER TOOLING

Tooling is the method of imprinting a design in leather by pressing the outline deep into the leather with a smooth metal-edged tool. The background is stippled to make the foreground design stand out more clearly. This is a type of embossing. Calf leather is most frequently used for tooling. Cowhide used by upholsterers will also tool.

LEATHER STAMPING

In leather stamping, the design is put on cowhide or kip with steel or brass dies which are struck with a wooden mallet making an imprint on dampened leather. (Most of the Mexican purses made for the tourist trade are the stamped variety.) When the leather dries, the design remains in the leather. Western-style belts can be made by this method.

LEATHER CARVING

Cowhide and kip are the leathers used for carving. The design is cut into the leather with a leather carving tool. Dies of various types are then used to bevel, work the background and add such details as veins in leaves and markings on stems of flowers and plants. A three-dimensional effect is achieved since the designs are cut to a depth which makes this possible. The depth of the cut depends, of course, on the thickness of the leather. Western-style holsters, knife sheaths, saddles, purses and belts are the projects usually carved.

Since leather items are needed constantly in everyday living, leather craft is a practical as well as interesting home craft. It is clean, requires relatively few tools and its possibilities are practically unlimited. When one masters tooling and carving the use of dye and gold leaf add to the variety of possibilities. This is definitely one of the crafts one could do for half a lifetime and never know all about it.

TYPES OF LEATHER FOR LEATHER CRAFT

There are many types of leather. For tooling, calf is the best. However, cowhide such as is used by upholsterers comes in beautiful colors and is cheaper than calf. It can be bought by the pound in varying-sized pieces. It tools beautifully and can be used for coin purses, key cases, wallets, zipper brief cases and women's purses. It is cheaper by far than calf and is good leather on which to practice techniques.

Carving leather is either cowhide or kip which comes from the animal between the calf and cow stage. Kip is thinner than cowhide and is used for wallets, billfolds and coin purses. Cowhide is thick leather. Cowhide comes in varying thicknesses. Each sixty-fourth of an inch is termed an ounce. Thus five-ounce leather is five sixty-fourths of an inch thick. It comes only in natural color but can be dyed to almost any color with leather dyes. It is used to makes purses, holsters, knife sheaths, saddles, brief cases, belts and notebooks.

Lining leather of various thicknesses, colors and finishes come from several types of animals. Lining leather from sheep, capeskin (smooth), suède (soft-textured), skiver (very thin and smooth), pigtex (imitation pigskin finish) are available in many colors. Goat hide is used as lining leather. Lamb lining is thinner than sheep and comes in smaller hides. Pigskin is also a good lining leather.

Fur leathers are also available. Unborn calf makes beautiful billfolds and purses. Sheep woolskin is used for moccasins and jackets and vests where the woolly finish is desired for warmth. Toy animals are also made from woolskin.

Enameling on Metal

Enameling on metal has been an art possible only in art schools and artist's studios, for the most part due to the fact that the kilns were large and required special wiring. Now small kilns have been developed and all-in-one kits are now available for use at home on the kitchen table or in the basement. Simple jewelry projects and small ash trays can be made in the small kilns. Thus an art activity formerly possible only for a few can be done by anyone who owns an electrical outlet and a work space.

Gem Cutting and Lapidary Work

In recent years there has been a great surge of interest in this field. Amateur gem cutters are working together in classes at natural history museums and in community centers. Many are setting up their own equipment in basement workshops. Compact gem-cutting equipment now available can be set up in limited spaces. Children and adults can enjoy this craft.

Such a craft has many ramifications. Families plan their vacations in areas where semiprecious and precious gem material can be picked up free by the zealous and not easily discouraged. Walk along the shores of Lake Superior any time of day and you will see the "rock hounds" searching the beaches and wading into the shallow water in search of thomsonite, Lake Superior agates and other interesting rocks. Petoskey stones are always eagerly looked for along the shores of Lake Michigan near Petoskey, Michigan. In the Western states, agate, petrified wood and other types of semiprecious gem materials are the treasures to be found.

Once the material is collected and then polished to perfection, many lapidaries turn to jewelry making in order to show off their polished treasures to the best advantage. One interest leads to another. In this as in many arts and crafts, the future is as bright as the past or present. There is always something more interesting to do tomorrow than there was today. Life is always brighter when the future is full of promises. When an individual reaches the stage when only the past is of interest and the future is full of uncertainties and fears, life has indeed lost its savor.

Woodworking

Lucky indeed is the child whose father owns woodworking tools and has a workbench set up in the garage or basement. Such a child knows the fun of making something along with Dad. Such a child soon learns to recognize the possibilities in a discarded apple, peach or orange crate. From such a treasure a fellow can make all kinds of stuff necessary to keep a boy happy. One time it may be buildings or bridges for the model train. Another time in combination with scrap lumber and corrugated cardboard, the boxes may be used to construct a tree house, a fort or a clubhouse.

With these tools, major as well as minor home repairs are effected.

Camping equipment, frames for high-fidelity speakers, furniture, lawn furniture, birdhouses or anything dear to the heart of Mom, Dad or the kids can be constructed.

Any tools which make possible the execution of ideas develop ingenuity and increase the efficiency and self-sufficiency of an individual. After a time nothing seems impossible. If one can't afford to buy it but can make it, many things which might be out of reach of the family pocketbook are possible. All the fun of using it and all the pleasure of bragging about it to visitors are added to the joy of creating it. There is no feeling comparable to that which comes when you've made something with your own hands.

Ceramics

As with metal enameling, ceramics as a home craft is now possible. Many persons who joined a class in a community center or art school have purchased their own equipment and set up shop in their basements or garages. Here again is an art in which children and adults can participate together. The products can be functional pieces such as bowls, dishes, cups, vases or platters which can be turned out by hand or on a potter's wheel or modeled and sculptured pieces which serve as decoration only.

Clay is a satisfying medium with which to work. Clay enthusiasts find it a very relaxing, strain-and-stress-reducing material with which to engage in creative play.

Families which cannot afford the equipment of kiln and potter's wheel or do not have the space which is needed to work this rather messy material can still enjoy the fun of creating in clay by using the non-drying form of clay of the Plasticine variety. This clay works well in the hands but is not dirty. The finished products are not permanent, but all the satisfying and relaxing fun of working with the clay is there.

Weaving

Some homes have their weaving rooms where a small and large loom are available for all types of weaving. This is a practical as well as relaxing form of creative activity. The actual mechanics of weaving are not difficult. The blind can weave as well as the sighted. Children and adults find the activity fascinating. The products are practical and functional. Check to see if there is a weavers' guild in your home town. Any member will gladly give you information and a demonstration which will help you in determining if this is the craft for you.

Sewing

Woe to the girl who is raised in a home that does not own a sewing machine, where all articles of clothing are bought ready-made and any repairs or alterations are done by the neighborhood dressmaker or tailor.

Clothing made in the home is far cheaper, in most cases, than that of comparable quality sold in stores. Nothing is more satisfying to the home dressmaker or tailor than the fun of taking an old garment, ripping it apart, cleaning or laundering the material and making it over into a beautiful and useful article of wearing apparel for some member of the family. Outmoded winter coats are cut down and made into children's jackets. Dad blossoms out in a fancy shirt made by Susie or Mom and is the fashion plate of the square dance. Little sister wears dresses with fancy embroidery which look costly and actually were most inexpensive to make.

Even the boys find use for the sewing machine to fashion sails for their boats or coverings for their Indian tepees. New and relatively uncomplicated sewing machines on the market now do everything but cut out the material. The possibilities in this practical and satisfying home art are now almost unlimited.

The daughter who learns to make many of her own clothes becomes the efficient housewife who can keep her children attractively and well outfitted on a limited clothing budget. The boy in the family who can sew a straight seam need not feel his masculinity is in question. No one ever need apologize for possessing any skill.

Home Artists

Grandma Moses has given the older citizens a wonderful lift, art-wise. Many retired golden-agers are turning to painting for fun and relaxation. People who thought they couldn't possibly do so are now finding they can turn out creditable paintings. Whether or not their canvases ever hang in the art museums is not important. What the actual business of painting does for the individual is the important thing. One amateur painter says: "When I begin to paint time stops for me. I forget my troubles, I forget my aches and pains. I forget to eat lunch. It's wonderful fun!"

Whether one creates in finger paints, oils, water colors, pastels, charcoal, pen and ink or crayons, the satisfaction is the same. Family members of any age will find this is a fascinating activity. One can work at home, carry his makeshift easel to the woods, to the back yard or out on the tenement fire escape. If the talent and urge are there, the artist's eye sees beauty of design, color or motion in almost any direction he turns his eyes. Indoors, outdoors, summer, fall, winter or spring the artist sees something worthy to record on his canvas or drawing paper. This art never palls. There is always a tomorrow. There is always something different and wonderful to see. There is always something new to learn.

Crocheting and Knitting

In some European countries children learn to crochet or knit before they go to school. Some become so adept they can knit in the dark while they attend movies or watch television. Beautiful articles of wearing apparel, sweaters, dresses, baby garments, lace of all types for use on many household articles are turned out in volume at costs far below the almost prohibitive prices charged in stores for hand-knit and hand-crocheted articles.

This is a practical skill well worth cultivating since it can be put to use in so many ways. The equipment is inexpensive, the variety of yarns increases year by year as the new synthetic yarns come on the market. It requires no special work space. A knitter or crocheter can apply her art when ill in bed, resting after a day's labors, while visiting with friends or when traveling. Hand-knit and crocheted items are always welcome gifts, cherished not only for their beauty but for the thought and time put into the article by the maker. Do not believe that this is only a woman's art. Men crochet and knit. Surgeons have taken up one or the other of these crafts to keep their fingers limber. Sailors on the old windjammers knit or crocheted to fill the long hours at sea. Men who find this craft as relaxing as women are not the sissy type by any means.

Bobbin or Pillow Lace

This ancient Old World craft is another which is being revived in this country. It is now possible to get books on the craft and to join classes where it is taught. Looking more complicated to make than in reality it is, the lace turned out is well worth the effort it takes. Those familiar with the bobbin lace turned out in Brussels by women who work on the sidewalks or in stores there know how unusual this type of beautiful lace is. Its history is a fascinating one cutting across political, religious and commercial lines. It is a lace made in many parts of the world and with many kinds of threads. Bobbin lace makers find the history, the variety of patterns, the different types of equipment as fascinating as the application of the art itself. Since in the Old World it is a craft learned by children at a young age, it is another of the wonderful crafts possible for families to do together.

Whittling

Contrary to all beliefs, one does not need to be a tobacco chewer to be a whittler or wood carver. Children and adults of either sex can learn to whittle or carve. At first, the only equipment needed for whittling is a block of soft wood (balsa, sugar pine or white pine) and a good sharp jackknife with a large and small blade. There are many good books available which will give helpful hints. Whittlers will enjoy visiting the craft centers in North Carolina and the Smoky Mountain areas where it is possible to watch men and women at work. When one sees how beautiful even the simplest carving of a bird or animal is, it gives one the courage to try his hand.

Bas-relief wood carving is another art which is almost a lost one. Architectural wood carvers are hard to find. Many working now are the old-timers who never have to worry about being forced to retire, so few replacements are there to take their places. Wood carving sets are not expensive. Many carvers haunt auctions which are held when old houses are being torn down and buy the paneling which graced the walls of these fine old mansions. Cherry, walnut, mahogany of a quality now difficult to find are soon turned into exquisitely carved plaques worthy of being hung in museums. However, one need not go to such lengths to find suitable wood. One retired carver has used maple breadboards both round and rectangular in shape which he has purchased in the ten-cent store for less than a dollar. He has designed and carved them, creating beautiful pieces.

True Crafts *vs.* Fad Crafts

The possibilities for a family program in arts and crafts are almost limitless. One word of caution, however, should be given here. Do not confuse arts and crafts or group them in the same field with the fad-type so-called craft kits. For example a recent fad was rhinestone jewelry which required only cementing a bit of glittering glass on a bit of metal attractively and sometimes not so attractively made into a piece of costume jewelry. Suddenly everyone was "making" rhinestone jewelry. Within a few months the world seemed flooded with it. Gradually the fad began to fade and before it completely died another took its place. Such assembly kits are not true crafts. People soon tire of making the things because there is practically no challenge except that of putting something together. It requires little creativity, practically no ingenuity and very often involves a considerable outlay of money considering how long the fad will last.

While families may want to indulge themselves occasionally in this kind of activity, the wiser method is to spend money carefully on the kinds of tools and craft supplies that bring the most satisfaction over a longer period. Invariably the crafts which have stood the test of time are the most practical and the most satisfying.

5

Fun with Family Camping

If yours is the type of family which rises eagerly and nobly to the challenge requiring ingenuity, camping should be on your program of family fun. For if ever there was an activity which is a constant challenge to the ability of the individual to adjust himself to his environment and, in some instances, modify and shape it to the end which brings him comfort and satisfaction, camping is that activity.

The average person lives in a snug house of wood or stone where windows which shut out the weather or invite it in are adjusted with a minimum of effort; where light and heat are produced with the flick of a switch; where modern bathing and toilet facilities are readily available; where the furniture necessary for daily living (eating, sleeping, cooking) is taken for granted; where food supplies of all kinds are within a few minutes' driving distance; where gadgets and appliances to perform every manner of task necessary to comfortable living are at hand. Camping, which offers none of these advantages, is a dare to which only the stalwart and brave respond.

The surprising part of it all is the manner of persons who prove to be the brave and stalwart. Are they only the athletic, hard-muscled, he-man type of individual who deep-breathes his way through life, pounding his manly chest and emitting Tarzan-like cries? Indeed not. Visit a camping area and look carefully at the people there. You'll find them of all ages from babies to grandparents. They will be all shapes and sizes and all manner of person. There will be the balding, more-than-slightly paunched man (obviously a behind-the-desk man) fervently, if not always skillfully, going about camp-keeping duties chopping firewood, putting up tents, stretching tarpaulins or filling lanterns. You'll see women who look femininely glamorous even in their camp clothes efficiently and happily preparing the family meal over the charcoal grill or camp stove. If you stop to think about it, the people you see look like any miscellaneous group of people you'd

meet walking down Main Street. Except for their attire and the unusual tasks they are performing, they look like an ordinary crowd of people going about their business. They are no special breed of supermen and women.

What makes these people leave their comfortable homes with all the modern conveniences to vacation in state and federal park camping grounds, cook over a campfire, sleep on the ground with or without air mattresses or on hard camp cots, take their chances on weathering comfortably the cold, the heat, the downpours, and even severe storms in temporary shelters of canvas? Is it because such a vacation is less expensive than a hotel or resort type? Not necessarily. Some families invest considerable money in a camping outfit, buying every gadget the camp store tickles their vulnerable spots with. Is it their almost fanatical love of the out-of-doors? Not solely. Families might satisfy this interest in out-of-the-way spots where they could spend most of their waking hours out in the woods, near the water or in the mountain and still have the comfort and security of a cabin at night and during inclement weather. Is it love of adventure? Not wholly. People can find equally satisfying adventures without going to all the trouble of camping out.

Ask these campers and their answers will be varied. Some will tell you they camp because they meet so many unusual people. Campers, they will tell you, are friendly folks delightful to have as neighbors, eager to be pleasant yet careful not to intrude on their neighbors' privacy or to interfere in anyway with their comforts. They are a special lot more careful of the feelings of others with a smaller percentage of bores, nuisances and pests that you would find in a group of equal size in any ordinary cross-section of population. This fact may be due partly to the fact that the everyday business of camping keeps the campers so occupied that they have little time to be petty or bored, but most campers would say that people who camp are an especially nice group of people.

Another reason why families take to camping is to satisfy the same spirit of adventure that their pioneer ancestors did. They want to prove to themselves that despite soft city living they are still as hardy in spirit as their forefathers and can endure and even enjoy the hardships of outdoor living along with the fun. If they are fair, they will point out that theirs is only a temporary adventure and is backed by the security of being able to turn back to their comfortable homes when it is over whereas their ancestors, for the most part, could only go forward or die in the attempt.

Whether campers admit it or not, there is the threat of the possibilities of impending war in the recesses of their mind. Camping out is a kind of practice session for the preservation of life following an attack. Campers have the doubtful comfort and assurance that they could manage somehow if the horrible necessity presented itself.

Whatever the guess about the psychology which motivates families who go camping, the fact remains that people do go. They love the challenge of it. They admit to the fun of it. And that is our chief concern here—the fun aspects of camping. They will tell you that because camping presents many real situations, it is of interest to family members of all ages. It is one of the activities which teen-age family members enjoy. It presents so many situations it is impossible to become bored. The task of everyday living takes on new meaning not only because the manner in which it is performed is so different, but because the difference between comfort and discomfort often lies in the degree of care and skill and the faithfulness to duty with which the task is performed. A camper has to be careful to select a good camp site which offers protection from insects, falling branches, sudden floods or other threats to comfort and safety. One must be skillful with the ax to escape serious injury while performing the duty of chopping the firewood which will be used to cook the food or provide warmth against the cool of the evening. One must certainly be skillful at the cooking fire or stove if he does not wish to have to satisfy his hunger with charred or tasteless food. There is no corner restaurant handy to run to if the dinner is ruined by a careless or unskilled hand. One must be faithful to duty and perform regularly the tasks which provide the comforts which make the camping experience enjoyable and pleasant. The camper who fails to get in enough firewood and chop it to size for its various functions and store it where it will remain dry may find himself in need of a fire to dry his rain-soaked clothes and to warm his chilled body with no dry firewood on hand. The camper who is not interested or is just too tired to trench his tent properly on a dry day may find himself awakened by the wet creeping uncomfortably into his sleeping bag and flooding his dry clothes supply. Unlike tasks in the city which can be put off until another day by the procrastinator without causing him to suffer discomfort, the tasks about the camp leave no such leeway.

If he does not cache his food properly it is open to attack by insects or animals, subject to spoilage by rain and hot weather (a serious problem where stores are not readily available for replacement).

The camper must plan carefully in advance so that he is carrying all the equipment necessary to comfortable camping. Some left-behind items can be substituted for easily but the ax, the extra blanket, the ropes or some equally indispensable items are not easily replaced nor do they have satisfactory substitutes. Nothing does the work of an ax. No seasoning takes the place of salt in food. The left-at-home rubbers or boots won't protect shoes from becoming soaked through and leaving the wearer cold and uncomfortable. It would be a challenge to anyone's ingenuity to provide a satisfactory substitute for rubbers if going barefooted is not feasible or safe.

Camping is a disciplined kind of living. It imposes its demands, levying its punishment for laxity and failure to perform with discomfort, pain and misery and rewarding the faithful with comfort, joy and deep satisfaction. Because of this, it is wise to begin slowly and carefully to build the family up to a camping vacation. The family needs to go into training for any prolonged camping trip just as any athlete has to train for the rigors of a season of vigorous and rugged sports. Don't expect to take a city family and plunge them into a camping vacation without careful preparation and training and have it turn out to be the most successful vacation the family ever had. It could be the worst they ever endured—never to be forgotten, never to be tried again.

TRAINING FOR CAMPING

Start the family out easily. Begin by spending week-ends in a cabin in a state or national park within easy driving distance of home. Even life in a snug but meagerly equipped cabin can be rugged to the city-bred. If the family members learn to enjoy life without electricity and indoor plumbing, like cooking over a fire, being out in the quiet dark woods at night and going to bed early, go on to the next step. Try living out in the open for a week-end, sleeping out in sleeping bags, bathing in the old swimming hole, cooking over a campfire or on a camp stove. If the family responds agreeably to this and suggests repeat engagements it's time then to think of a prolonged family camping trip and the need to buy camping equipment.

The family graduates to lean-to or tent living first for a week-end, then for a couple of weeks. A camping team needs to be built up and trained as carefully as any football or baseball team. There is a role for each family member to play in making the camping experience successful. Certain skills can be learned and practiced at home. Handling an ax properly and safely is best learned at home. Pitching a tent in jig time in a high wind or under other adverse conditions is a skill to be learned before the necessity for getting a shelter up in time is imperative. Pitching a tent can be practiced in one's back yard often enough so that it can be done easily, quickly and skillfully in daylight or semidarkness. There may be a time on the camping trip when this skill means the difference between a drenching or a dry shelter under a tent roof, a night sleeping out in the open or in the relative comfort of a tent shelter.

Taking the tent down and being able to stow it quickly is important, too. You may have to break camp hurriedly one day before a storm breaks. Practice in this procedure pays off then.

Cooking skills over wood fire or charcoal grill should be practiced at family picnics in near-by parks or in the back yard where failures resulting from inexperienced cooking can be supplemented by provisions from the family kitchen. Out in the woods miles from markets and extra food supplies is no place to begin to learn about cooking out.

Sleeping out at night in the tent pitched in the back yard is good training for camping out. Familiarity eliminates many unnecessary, unpleasant camping experiences which could ruin camping forever as a family project.

Week-end or home practice sessions soon separate the campers from the noncampers. On a family camping trip everyone must want to camp. One dissatisfied member who came because he had to and not because he wanted to can make life miserable for everyone. Camping necessitates close living. The whole family may be housed in one tent. One protesting miserable member can ruin the good time of a whole tentful of people.

Be understanding of this person. Remember that not everybody likes the same things. While we try to train children to be polite and obedient and to attempt to be agreeable under circumstances they find it hard to be enthusiastic about, rugged outdoor living is not the activity to demand such behavior. It is better to leave that member at home or make other arrangements for him than to force him to accompany the family on the camping expedition. Never the twain shall meet— the dedicated camper and the violently opposed noncamper. Their minds are poles apart. It is better to recognize the differences and accept them than to attempt to convert or force the individual into submission. It would be better to abandon the whole idea of a family camping trip than force the issue for there is no good to be gained. Only a miserable time for the others is likely to be the result.

PRECAMP PREPARATION

Camping, like any hobby, can plunge the unwary and uninitiated into a splurge of expensive buying. Before purchasing anything, read some good books on camping. Consult your camper friends about the pitfalls of unnecessary buying. Make lists. Check these lists several times. If a particular piece of equipment or a tool can be made to serve more than one purpose, that is the one to buy because you not only save money by this procedure but conserve space as well. Discard the items which are only one-shot tools, if you can substitute another which serves more than one function.

Don't try to live in a camp as luxuriously as you do at home. You can be clean, comfortable and well fed without filling a trailer with extra equipment which may add to your comfort for a few hours but which may afford you more discomfort in the added time it takes to pack. Remember, too, that the more equipment you carry, the more space you need. Imprudence not only adds to the expense of the camping kit but may necessitate the extra expense of the purchase of a trailer to house it.

Even with careful list-planning and prudent buying (and don't be too proud to watch want ads for sales of used camping equipment) a good camping outfit is not cheap. Yet if pro-rated over the period of years which the family will be using it and compared with the cost of housing a family nightly in a cabin or motel it will not be costly at all. A tent with careful usage and storage will last twenty years. Its initial cost is less than the price of housing your family in a cabin or motel for only a few nights. A camp stove can be used time and again on picnics and back-yard cook-outs. It will come in handy as an auxiliary stove at home when the electric power goes off and the electric range is not usable at meal time. Air mattresses and sleeping bags will make sleeping on the floor an adventure for the children when a large dose of house guests overflows the sleeping accommodations and spills out into the rest of the house. If it is summer, the tent can be pitched in the back yard and add to the fun of the adventure for the younger guests.

Certain tools necessary for camping are the same as those used on many other occasions during the year and so may already be owned and need not be purchased.

MAKING THE CAMPING EQUIPMENT LIST

In making your camping list itemize everything you think you will need. Go over it carefully and eliminate the items you can do without or which can be substituted for by other items on the list.

Once you have evolved your minimum-maximum list go over it carefully again, underlining the items which you already own and need not buy. Now make a new list itemizing only the pieces of equipment which you need to buy. Don't go out and buy these all in one mad buying spree. Spread your buying over a period of weeks, watching for ads which offer bargain prices and want ads which list used items for sale. This method will be useful in many ways. First you have all the fun of planning and buying spread over a long period which keeps the family interest high. Each new piece of equipment purchased is like Christmas all over again. It is something to be admired, touched, practiced with and then put away with high hopes and suppressed excitement against the day it will be used. Secondly, your expenditures are spread over a longer period and fit better into your budget. Thirdly, since you are shopping unhurriedly you can take advantage of bargain prices. Fourthly, you will be revising your list as you go along, eliminating or adding to it as the case may be as new ideas on how to make equipment you might otherwise have bought come into being. This creativity and ingenuity will be another source of enjoyment which gives pleasure before the camping season begins and again when you put that invention to use in your camp.

Every family camps in its own way, some carrying a maximum, others a minimum, of equipment. The first attempts to take home with them and the second attempts to make a home in the woods in the simplest way possible and yet maintain some measure of comfort.

The lists of necessary equipment given here will probably not satisfy the experienced campers. Each has long since evolved his own list to suit his special method of camping. For the neophyte family campers who need help in assembling their gear, the lists given here can prove helpful. The inexperienced camper should study some good camping books, write a few lists and then consult with friends who have camped. The most helpful hints come from campers who have just finished a session. They will know good places within your section of the country to camp and which ones to avoid. They will be more than glad to pass along suggestions—their pet tricks which they have learned by experience make camping fun.

Camping equipment falls into several classifications each of which will be listed here and discussed at some length. The classifications are: housing, sleeping, clothing, housekeeping, tools, food and cooking.

Housing

It goes without saying that whatever equipment you buy is limited not only to what you can afford but to the quantity which you can pack into and on the top of your auto. If this does not provide enough space you will have to allow the excess to spill over into a two-wheeled trailer.

In any event, a tent for housing your family is necessary. If storage space between camping sessions is a problem it may be more prudent if more expensive over a period of years to rent rather than purchase a tent. The size of the tent depends upon the size of the family. A nine-by-nine umbrella tent with a canvas floor will accommodate four sleepers. This is an easy tent to erect and take down. If your family is larger it might be easier to have two small tents than one large

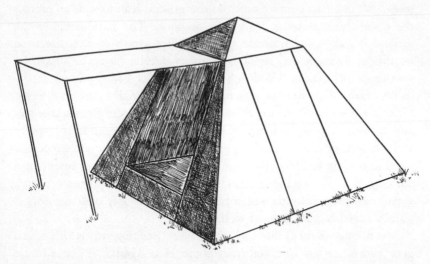

enough to accommodate the entire family because of the difficulty of erecting, knocking down and stowing a large tent.

A nine-by-twelve tarpaulin which is stretched and anchored to four trees to cover the cooking and eating area is another necessary piece of equipment. On good days the tarp is hung in a more or less horizontal position though it may be hung with some slope to allow shade from the noon and afternoon sun which is the time shade would be most welcome. On inclement days, the tarp may be stretched between two

trees with one part coming down to the ground lean-to style to protect the cook and the diners from rain or wind. The part touching the ground is staked and fastened securely. Since a tarp of such size is so flexible in its use it may be hung in many different ways to afford the maximum protection. See sketch for rigging for bad days.

Ponchos which protect you from the rain by day can double for night use under the sleeping bags. They are used under the blanket roll and again on top of the blankets (if you are sleeping out in the open) and are necessary pieces of camping equipment. They are especially good as they have more than one use. In all camping equipment purchasing, if it is possible to purchase one piece of equipment which serves two purposes rather than two which serve only one, not only is money saved but bulkage as well.

It is not necessary to buy special blankets. Bedding which will afford good protection can be taken from home. Here again it is better to use what is on hand than to go out and buy special equipment for camping. Your camping kit will cost less if you can fill in with already owned items. The problem of storage of camping equipment between trips is not so serious either.

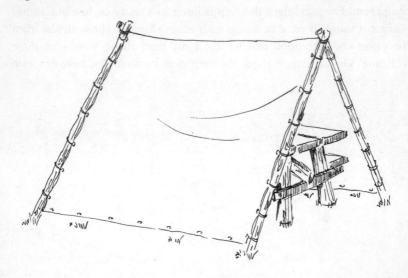

If sleepers must have pillows, it is better to carry foam-rubber-filled pillows which do not suffer from dampness as down or feather pillows do. Make your own by buying scrap rubber and shredding it to half-inch bits and filling pillow ticks made from any sturdy material you may have at home. You can make them to size to suit each individual camper at a minimum cost.

In addition to the tent the following equipment is necessary to the stability and erection of the tent:

1. Trenching shovel (a foxhole digger available in army surplus stores is suitable).
2. Sets of tent stakes:
   a. 4 wooden stakes (flat for sandy soil)
   b. 4 metal stakes for rocky soil (railroad spikes are good)
   c. 4 narrow metal stakes with teeth for sandy soil
   d. Extra sets of stakes for use with the tarpaulin
3. Reel of half-inch rope cut in six- to eight-foot lengths with the ends served with beeswax cord to prevent wasteful and hard-to-handle raveling. Also one fifty-foot length for rigging the tarpaulin on bad days.
4. Small ax which doubles as hammer for pounding in stakes.

Sleeping

Most campers find it more comfortable to sleep on air mattresses or camp cots than on the ground. Some prefer blanket rolls and others sleeping bags. Whichever you prefer, the important precaution to observe is to carry enough blankets to keep you warm. Nights in the open or in the mountains or woods can be very cold even in midsummer. Nothing makes a camper unhappier than to be cold in the night and have no way of getting warm except to get up, put on more clothing and maybe even start a fire. Plenty of blankets will eliminate these unnecessarily unpleasant sleepless nights.

If you buy sleeping bags, check the minimum temperatures at which they are effective. If you plan to camp in mountains or during the colder months, you will want bags affording the maximum protection. Bags which open across the bottom as well as down the length can be opened for airing and thus are better bags.

Clothing

Utility and versatility are the most important considerations in the selection of the clothes to be taken on a camping trip. Utility involves the business of selecting garments which will serve the wearers on warm as well as cold days, dry as well as wet. Versatility implies that some types of clothes will not only be suitable for several kinds of weather conditions but will afford maximum protection against the insects and underbrush. They should be the type that can be easily laundered and kept in a clean, presentable condition without benefit of electric iron and pressing board.

If layer dressing is practiced, the necessity to take great quantities of clothing is eliminated. For example on cold mornings the camper might begin the day with a pair of walking shorts under a pair of jeans or wool slacks, a tee shirt under a sweat shirt which is being worn under a wool jacket. As the day progresses and the sun takes over and warms the atmosphere, layer after layer is eliminated as comfort demands. The camper need not rush back to the tent and rummage in his duffel and change to other clothes.

Wool clothing is lighter in weight, warmer and more versatile than leather. A discarded sweater can be knotted around the wearer's waist by the sleeves and carried comfortably and easily in this manner. A leather jacket cannot.

Tightly woven cotton tee shirts launder easily, look presentable without ironing and are comfortable in all kinds of weather when layer dressing is practiced.

Bearing utility and versatility in mind, we offer the following list of clothing as most suited and necessary to comfortable camping:

Hooded all-wool or half-cotton, half-wool sweat shirt
Wool sweaters (long-sleeved)
Light rain jacket to be worn over wool clothing fills many needs
Wool trousers, corduroy pants, denim trousers

Cotton socks, wool socks, and half-wool, half-cotton socks
Cotton handkerchiefs
Cotton underclothing
Cotton tee shirts
Sleeping clothes, light cotton variety and warm wool or cotton flannel

Wet Weather Clothing

Ponchos are suitable for short people. Tall campers will have to roll up trousers if wearing a poncho to keep their trousers from becoming soaked by rivulets of water which run off the poncho in a heavy downpour. Ponchos are better in the underbrush than lighter raincoats. They are more comfortable as they allow the air to circulate and the hiker is not so apt to get all steamed up as he does in a plastic-type raincoat. Then, too, ponchos have another use. They are placed on the ground under the outdoor sleepers and also over the top blanket to protect sleepers from dew or rain. (See sleeping-out hints in section on camping techniques.)

Rubbers and light rain boots will be helpful in light rains but in heavy downpours feet will get wet anyway. Waterproofed shoes offer the most protection.

Packing Clothing

A duffel is the best type of equipment for packing camp clothing. Each camper has his own duffel and packs and unpacks his own clothing. A camping tip passed on by an experienced camper is to prepare the duffel for easy unpacking by sewing a heavy zipper the length of the seam of the duffel. (Zipper duffels can be purchased but do not open at the top.) The duffel is then packed from the top opening but is unpacked through the zipper opening since invariably the piece of clothing desired at the moment is always at the bottom of the kit, necessitating the removal of everything on top.

It is advisable to have a dirty clothing bag so that all soiled clothing can be separated from the clean, eliminating the unsanitary business of packing soiled with clean clothing. Since dirty clothing is already separated and gathered together in one place washdays are simplified.

Camp Laundry

Washing may be done in camp using cold water detergents if water is not to be heated. A pot of boiling water can be used to warm up a bucket of cold water for washing purposes. Campers old enough to do their own laundry should do it. With a large family where soiled clothing piles up in a hurry, it is smart to allow time for a visit to town and the self-serve laundry where several loads of soiled clothing can be washed and dried in a relatively short time. While Mother and one of the older children perform the laundry duties, Father may take the younger children on a shopping expedition to replenish diminishing food supplies. The day in town after days of camping will be a welcome change. Later before going back to camp the entire family may enjoy a special treat together—a soda, a movie or a trip about the town which includes some of the special sights.

Hand washing at camp can be done in a pail. A small washboard will be a welcome aid. For drying wet sweaters, tee shirts or wool jackets and shirt (whether wet from being laundered or from the rain) put the washline through the sleeves of these items and pin in place after washline is stretched. The wind whipping through will leave the clothing fluffy and smooth almost as if they had been pressed. Do not dry woolen things in the hot sun, of course.

Housekeeping

Housekeeping duties go on in camp just as they do in a home, although somewhat simplified and requiring far less equipment. Your minimum list should include:

Cleaning equipment

Broom (Small-size one will do.)

Dustpan

Dishpan (plastic). A large kettle can be used for dishes, but the dishpan will serve as a laundry pan as well.

Dish drainer (Dishes are washed in warm soapy water, placed in drainer and rinsed by pouring scalding water over them. Cover with a clean dish towel and allow to air-dry.)

Washline, spring-type clothespins, detergent, small washboard

Dish towels, cellulose sponges, soapy steel wool pads

Pail

Cooking

Cooking pans need not be specially purchased equipment, but may be those used at home. You will take fewer pans than you own to save packing space but those you take should include:

Two cast-iron skillets with tightly fitting lids, one medium-sized and one large

Cast-iron Dutch oven for stews or pot roasts (The large-sized frying pan will serve in this capacity.)

Bale-handled kettle, various-sized saucepans with lids

Can, jar and bottle opener (Better have a spare of each put away in a safe place.)

Toasting racks which can be used for toasting bread, broiling wieners, hamburgers, chicken, etc.

Long-handled fork, spoon and knife (barbecue set)

Bread board

Dipper

Knives, paring, boning and bread

Pot holders, cotton work gloves

Rectangular griddle will not take much packing space and will be useful for all frying—griddle cakes, chops, bacon, eggs, fish, etc.

Collapsible charcoal grill

Two-burner bottled gas or gasoline stove

Reflector oven (See directions for using under camp techniques section devoted to campfire cookery.)

Piece of heavy sheet metal about two feet square placed over a camp stove keeps pots clean when cooking and protects the fireplace on bad days.

Food Storage

Food keeps better and is better protected from insects and rodents if stored in tin cans with tight-fitting covers. Save coffee cans and other cookie and potato chip cans during the year for this purpose.

In packing put foodstuffs into cardboard cartons which are also labeled as to contents. If cans are labeled on top as well as sides (by a china-marking pencil or a Magic Marker available in stationery stores) it will be easy to identify contents of cans when they are in cartons. Try to keep like foods in one carton so that you will not have to go through the contents of several when you are preparing a meal. For example, if you keep seasonings and condiments together in one place, canned goods in another, dry foods and cereals in their own box, the preparation of meals will be easier.

Food Refrigeration

A portable icebox is valuable if you are camping where ice is available. The refrigerator is useful in keeping food fresh in the car as you travel from one place to another. Get the size which is practical for your family. It is a good investment. It will be useful during the year for family picnics and excursions and for party times when you need to keep quantities of bottled drinks cold.

A camp cooler keeps food fresh and protects it from animals as well. A new garbage can with a bale handle which locks the lid in place makes an excellent cooler. If camping near a mountain stream or any source of cold water place the cooler in the water and place rocks around it and some in it to keep it from being tipped over by the force of the water. Another method of cooling food is to dig a pit deep enough to accommodate the can. Cover the pit with a piece of tarp weighted or pegged down. This will not refrigerate the food but will keep fruits, vegetables and smoked meats cool and fresh.

Never use food you have any question about. Better to waste the food than to get food poisoning and have to find a hospital in a hurry.

Tools and Supplies

Since what you don't have with you you may have to make, tools are a very important part of the camp kit. Carpenter tools should include:

A hammer, screwdriver kit with interchangeable tips, pliers and a small but effective combination saw.

Ax—The double-bitted ax is the best woodsman's ax but too dangerous for the ordinary camper. The hunter's ax can double as a hammer for pounding stakes and nails, is lighter and can be carried in a leather cover and worn in the belt on the trail. A camp ax is not to be mistaken for a hatchet which is not so effective nor efficient a tool as an ax. A sixteen- or seventeen-inch-handled ax is a good size for a camper.

Sharpening stone—An ax to be effective must be very sharp.

Extra wedges—Carry wedges and check ax handle regularly before using to be sure the head is tight on the handle.

Machete—A machete which can be carried in a leather sheath is a good tool around the camp site. It can be used for clearing weeds as well as cutting light wood for the campfire. It makes a good tool to carry on the trail for trail clearing. Recommended is one with an eighteen-inch blade which is broad at the hilt and does not come to a narrow point.

Supplies—Assorted nails and screws, heavy staples for securing the tent to a tent platform, clothesline, spring-type clothespins, a coil or two of stove wire will all come in handy at one time or another.

Food Supplies

The food supplies you carry depend upon the eating likes and dislikes of your family, the menus you plan (in advance) and the places where you expect to camp. In other words, the menus you plan will feature foods which your family members like. Secondly, if you are planning to camp in remote places away from urban supermarkets your choice of canned meats, canned prepared foods, etc. is not so great in the crossroads general store and the prices will be higher on most items. To stay within your food budget, it is wiser to shop at home in advance selecting foods you will need for your prepared-in-advance menus. Fresh fruits and vegetables and meats can be purchased near the camping site so that you will need to keep them refrigerated only for brief periods before consuming them.

Part of the fun of camping is being sufficient unto yourselves and "making do" with what you have on hand. The more palatable your foods under these circumstances the prouder and more self-satisfied you can be of your ability to adapt to the outdoor situation efficiently and pleasantly. Therefore, it is wise to plan a series of meals ahead and buy in cans or boxes what you will be needing. The supplies can be supplemented with the fresh foods which you buy along the way.

Good campers can get along with dried or canned milk. Dried milk when mixed in advance (with safe water) and then left to stand under cold or refrigerated conditions is quite like the regular milk especially if it is aerated thoroughly before drinking. A chocolate variety is now available for a welcome change.

Carry with you glass jars with tight-fitting screw-on lids or plastic containers with lids. Butter, bacon, oleo and other such foods which you will keep in the camp icebox will need such protection. As the ice melts your food will sometimes be submerged in the water. If the food is in jars the cold water will help to keep it cold but will not spoil it.

Listed below under their various classifications are a number of canned and prepared food which are readily available. Suggested menus using these foods follow. The list can serve only as a guide in your purchasing as you must consider your family's taste in food. The size of the cans you buy depends upon the number in your family. Buy the size which your family will consume at one meal. Leftovers can be dangerous when refrigeration is not so efficient and dependable as at home.

Another way to determine which foods you should buy for your camping expedition is for you to list all your family's favorite meals. Eliminate those dishes which require elaborate combinations of foods which would not be practical to take with you or would take too long in preparing. Obviously you will not be preparing stuffed chicken, huge meat roasts or baked beans which require hours of baking. Make up your menus from your lists of favorites. Plan some meals that can be fixed in a jiffy for the days that are too hot to be leaning over a campfire or for times of inclement weather or impending darkness. On cool days you use the ones which require more time at the stove or campfire. You can then cook the stews and other long-cooking dishes.

Suggested Food Lists

CANNED MEATS AND FISH
Tuna
Salmon
Spam, Treet, etc.
Dried beef
Corned beef

CONDIMENTS
Catsup
Mustard
Salt
Pepper
Seasoned salt
Garlic salt
Dehydrated onions or onion salt
Dehydrated green peppers
Herbs you use often in cooking
Cinnamon

CANNED VEGETABLES
Pickled and plain beets
Red kidney beans
Kernel corn
Cream-style corn
Wax beans
Peas
Canned dried lima beans

CANNED SOUPS
Vegetable
Vegetable beef
Scotch broth
Cream of mushroom
Cream of chicken
Bean with bacon
Chicken noodle
Tomato

CANNED FRUITS
Grapefruit
Pineapple
Maraschino cherries

CANNED JUICES
Tomato
Tomato mixed with other
  vegetables
Pineapple
Orange
Grapefruit
Mixed citrus fruits

CANNED PREPARED FOODS
Corned beef hash
Roast beef hash
Spaghetti and meatballs
Ravioli
Roast beef in gravy
Baked beans

DESSERTS
Crackers (salted and Graham)
Cookies
Marshmallows

DRIED STAPLES

Minute rice
Minute potatoes
Spaghetti
Noodles
Flour
Sugar
Brown sugar
Powdered sugar
Soup concentrate (beef or chicken)
Cocoa or hot chocolate mix
Pancake flour
Prepared biscuit mix
Coffee
Tea

MISCELLANEOUS

Maple syrup
Peanut butter
Jellies and jams
Mayonnaise
French salad dressing

FRESH MEATS (WHICH YOU
BUY CLOSE TO YOUR CAMP SITE)

Bacon
Ground beef (used immediately)
Cut-up chicken (used immediately)
Cube steaks
Sirloin steak (special treat)
Pork or lamb chops (special treat)
Round steak

FRESH FOODS (BOUGHT CLOSE TO CAMP SITE)

Vegetables—carrots, lettuce, tomatoes, cucumbers, cabbage, corn on the
    cob, potatoes, onions, celery
Fruits (in season)—peaches, pears, apples, plums, berries, bananas,
    oranges
Cereal—prepared
Bread—rolls, sweet rolls, your favorite breads

Menu Suggestions

Suggestions given here are for breakfast, lunch and dinner. Each
group will include both elaborate-type and jiffy-fixed meals.

BREAKFAST MENUS (REGULAR STYLE)

1. Fruit juice
   Bacon and egg (favorite style)
   Toast with butter and jelly
   Beverage
2. Fresh fruit (orange, sliced or whole peach, banana)
   Flapjacks with maple syrup, jelly or jam
   Bacon
   Beverage

3. Cereal with sliced banana
   French toast with syrup or jelly
   Bacon
   Beverage
4. Fruit or fruit juice
   Hot cereal (your favorite)
   Bacon fried crisp and cut up in small pieces and
   scrambled with eggs
   Beverage
5. Fruit or fruit juice
   Little pig sausages
   Bohemian fried bread
   (Make a batter of eggs, salt, milk and flour. Dip bread
   in batter and fry. Serve with syrup or jelly.)
6. Fruit or fruit juices
   Bacon and scrambled eggs
   Cinnamon toast
   Beverage
7. Fruit or fruit juices
   Fried fresh-caught fish
   Toast
   Beverage

(JIFFY STYLE)

1. Fruit juice
   Dry cereal with milk
   Toast with butter and jelly
   Beverage
2. Fresh fruit
   Peanut butter or jelly sandwich
   Beverage

LUNCHEON MENUS (REGULAR STYLE)

1. Your favorite soup
   Eggs scrambled with cottage cheese
   Bread and butter
   Fruit and cookies
   Beverage
2. Creamed chipped beef (made with dried milk)
3. Tuna fish salad made with tuna, celery tops and stalk,
   hard cooked eggs, grated onion mixed with mayonnaise

Sliced tomatoes
Fruit cup and cookies
Beverage

4. Scotch broth or vegetable soup
   Cucumber and tomato sandwiches
   Some mores (toasted marshmallows placed with a square
   of chocolate bar between two Graham crackers)
   Beverage

5. Spam or Treet cut into cubes and heated in creamed
   sauce made with cream of mushroom or cream of
   chicken soup to which chopped fried onions have
   been added. Serve on cooked minute rice.
   Tomato, lettuce salad or tossed salad
   Fruit and cookies
   Beverage

6. Chili and crackers
   Carrot and celery sticks
   Fruit
   Beverage

(JIFFY STYLE)

1. Sandwiches
   Sliced tomatoes
   Fruit
   Beverage

2. Fruit juice
   Hot canned spaghetti and meatballs
   Celery or carrot sticks
   Fruit and cookies
   Beverage

(DINNER MENUS)

See Chapter XV, "Family Fun on Vacations," for dinner menu
suggestions, as well as breakfasts and lunches.

CAMPING TRICKS AND TECHNIQUES

You will have insect repellent to rub on your skin and to spray on
your clothes and in the tent, but flies will come around your table

while you are eating and be bothersome. No one knows why this fly chaser works in keeping flies away, but campers find it a simple, effective device for eliminating flies around the eating area. Stretch a piece of twine above the length of the table. Hang eight- or ten-inch pieces of string at foot intervals along the twine. Tie a small ball of cotton batting at the end of the dangling strings. These string and cotton gadgets waving in the breezes keep the area clear of flies. Try this on your screen door at home or on the netting covering your tent flap.

Bee and Wasp Trap

An effective trap can be made from a square milk carton. Cut slits down the sides of a milk carton starting the slits about two inches from the top and ending them about the same distance from the bottom. Put a portion of catsup or some other odorous sweet substance in the bottom of the carton. Close the carton at the top and push down gently until the slits open up making a Japanese lantern effect. The stuff inside will attract the bees. They will get their wings wet in the goo and then remain trapped inside the box as they cannot fly with wet wings. The box can be burned in the campfire and a new one constructed every day or whenever necessary.

Water Supply

When camping out in an area which does not have a water supply of which you are sure, the best method to insure safety is boiling. Halazone tablets for purifying water are available but leave an unpleasant taste.

For water storage, an army surplus five-gallon can (enameled inside) is an excellent and inexpensive container. The boiled water can be kept in quart bottles with screw caps in your refrigerator or cooler. Pour the water back and forth from one container to another before drinking. The aeration will take away the flat taste of boiled water.

Oven Baking over the Campfire

Two kinds of ovens are useful in campfire cookery. The reflector oven which is a triangular-shaped device with two reflecting surfaces and two side pieces to keep out cold air is placed to one side of the fire. The heat from the fire enters the open side and is reflected down on

the food to be baked. Experts can bake biscuits, cakes and casseroles in these ovens. In the sketch above you can see how easy it would be to construct your own. They may also be purchased in camp stores.

The other oven, a one-oven burner, such as is used over kerosene or wood stoves is inexpensive and extremely useful in performing many functions. It can be placed on top of the camp stove. Biscuits, casseroles, potatoes and other such foods can be baked in it. It is useful for heating up sweet rolls and for keeping prepared foods warm. Its one disadvantage is its size and the packing space it requires. However it can be filled up with many little things and thus the packing space is not wasted after all.

Selecting the Camping Site

If you are planning to camp at a public camping ground in a state or federal park, plan to arrive early in the afternoon particularly in the height of the vacation season when camp grounds are apt to be filled to near capacity. Coming early will give you a chance to look over the situation in broad daylight and help you find an available site that is best suited to your needs and tastes. With some experience, you will find the spot which satisfies your needs most conveniently may not be to your liking in other matters. For example, you might like a site convenient to the washrooms and drinking water but its convenience features are offset by the fact that your neighbors are a group of teen-agers on a camping trip. Unless you like your sack time flavored with giggles of the practical joker and disturbed by the outraged cries of the victims, you may end up choosing a less convenient but quieter camping spot. Other factors should be taken into consideration if you have a choice. Some suggestions follow. Your own tastes, however, will be the factors in your ultimate selection of a site.

1. Before making a final decision, stay near your chosen site a while before unpacking and settling down. You may notice things that you didn't see at first which may help you change your mind about your choice of sites. You may notice that while the location seems ideal it is a gathering place for the bug clan. Watch for swarms of insects. Notice if they seem to stay in one place. If they do, pitch your tent away from that place. Sometimes only a few feet makes the difference for the better.

2. Wait a while to see if this is a quiet or noisy spot. At first you may not be aware that the doors of the convenient washroom squeak and groan and bang with most annoying regularity.

3. Comfort and safety-wise, these are some of the considerations in selecting a camping site:

a. Try to find a level spot. It's no fun sleeping uphill.

b. Tree shade is cooler than sunlight, but watch for bugs in the air or rodent holes near the tree roots. They may be friendly creatures who like making night calls. Watch for dead branches in the tree you camp under. A falling branch on a tent roof is a dangerous missile.

c. If the area you are in is subject to downpours with resultant flash floods, place your tent with such possibilities in mind.

d. Watch for anthills. Don't put your tent on top of one!

e. Try to determine whether your spot gets the morning or afternoon sun. A hot tent in the morning is not the most comfortable spot when you want to sleep late.

f. Place your tent so that the back or side is to the prevailing wind so that campfire smoke will not blow into your tent and any bad weather will not come in through the flap.

4. If a camping ground is crowded, before pitching your tent in

desperation in the one spot that's available, ask the ranger or some of the campers if there are any other available areas in the same park. There may be another which is not too distant, is less crowded and will give you a wider choice of sites.

Setting-up Camp Procedures

After selecting a camp site, determine the exact spot you wish to set up your tent. Clean the ground on which the floor of your tent will rest with a broom clearing out all sticks and sharp stones. Remember to consider the prevailing wind directions. Get out the tent and all the equipment you need in setting it up, the stakes, ropes, ax, etc. When all is in readiness, erect the tent. While the final adjustments are being made, the business of trenching the tent should also be in progress. A trench should be dug all around the tent about a foot from it. Dig it about two or three inches wide and about as deep and you will have adequate protection from flooding in a sudden downpour.

When the tent is up, erect the tarpaulin. While this is going up, the rest of the family can unpack the other gear. When the housing arrangements are finished, you are all set up to live it up in the great out-of-doors.

In the event it is raining when it is time to set up the tent, the tent crew dons ponchos and proceeds with the erection of the tent while the rest of the family stays in the car. When the tent is up, the tarpaulin is then stretched into place according to rainy and bad weather methods, with one side dropped down to afford the best possible protection from the rain and wind. When this is in place, the rest of the family goes into action carrying out their duties. There is no sense in everybody getting wet.

Mosquito Netting Tent

Mosquito netting tents make sleeping out a more pleasant experience in areas where the winged varmints are overactive. For a mosquito net tent you will need four nine-foot lengths of mosquito netting which comes thirty-six inches wide and costs less than twenty cents per yard.

Sew each length together using binding tape along the seams for strength. The strip of tape which goes down the middle seam should be a foot longer at each end so that loops can be fashioned. It is to these loops that you will attach your tying ropes by which you erect your tent between trees. When all lengths are sewed together you will have a netting nine feet long and twelve feet wide. Since it is to look like a tent you will have to use about one foot at each end to close the tent ends. Suspend your tent as you would at your sleeping

site and fashion the ends so that you have a pup tentlike structure and stitch the ends shut.

At the sleeping site, suspend your tent between two trees over your sleeping bag or blanket roll. Tuck in both ends and one side under your ponchos. Crawl in under the other side and tuck it in before you get into your blankets for the night.

Blanket Roll

If you do not have a sleeping bag or jungle hammock, you can sleep out on a blanket roll. You will need several blankets and two ponchos. To make a comfortable bed proceed in this manner:

1. Pick your sleeping spot with an eye to trees conveniently placed to which you can tie your mosquito netting tent.

2. Sweep area clean of twigs and pick up any stones or debris which would make your bed uncomfortable.

3. Lay one poncho on the ground snap side down smoothing it carefully.

4. Cover this poncho with several layers of blankets which serve not only as a mattress but as a warmth layer as well.

5. Now come your blanket roll blankets. With your eye, find the center line of your mattress layer and then the quarter line which would be halfway between the center line and the outside edge. With this quarter-division line in mind, lay one blanket on your mattress so that the right-hand edge of the blanket length is on the quarter-division line on the right side and smooth the blanket carefully. Working from the other side, lay another blanket on top of the first so that its left-hand edge is on the left-side quarter-division line. Now lay on a third blanket and a fourth and more, if you think you will need them, alternating each as you did with the first two. In other words, the third is in the same position as the first, the fourth in the same position as the second. Now fold the right-hand blankets toward the left side and the left-hand blankets toward the right making an envelope-like structure. (It's easier to do than explain.) Try this at home several times so you can do it quickly and in the dark if necessary.

6. Now turn the foot of the blanket roll under so no cold air can sneak in that way.

7. Lay your second poncho on top of your blanket roll and snap it to the bottom poncho.

8. When you are ready to bed down for the night, slide feet first into your blanket envelope and tuck in your mosquito netting. Good night and sweet dreams.

First-Aid Equipment

A well-equipped first-aid kit is an absolute necessity in camping where professional medical care is miles away. Since even a minor injury can be a serious one under these conditions, it is safe and wise to have a well-equipped and adequate kit which is ready for any contingency.

Equipment should include:

Band-aids for small wounds

Tincture of methylate

Tweezers for slivers
Adhesive tape, wide width
Compress bandages (sterile) of several sizes
Vaseline
Eyewash
Applicators
Tongue depressors
Needles for removing slivers
Matches for sterilizing needles
Gauze bandages of several widths
Three-cornered bandage for sling or large-bandage purpose
Ace elastic bandages for sprains
Alcohol
Snake bite kit with new razor blades
Sterile cotton
Vaseline gauze packs for burns
Sunburn lotion
Tourniquet (Be sure to understand use of this before applying
  and proper procedure after application while taking victim
  to doctor.)
Minor illness remedies such as:
Aspirin
Laxatives
Thermometer for taking temperatures
Salt tablets for excessively hot days
Calamine lotion for poison ivy
Boric acid powder or prepared eyewash
Your favorite sick stomach settler

General Safety Techniques While Camping

1. Don't leave your prized possessions lying around in plain sight while you are away from camp. Lock your cameras in the car or put them out of sight in the tent. Your ax and other camping equipment like lanterns and other easily picked-up equipment should be put

away before you leave camp for any time. Out of sight, out of temptation's way, is the rule to follow.

2. When going off on a long hike, leave word with someone which direction you are going and how long you expect to be gone. An accident on the trail may prevent your return. Help will reach you faster and more easily if you've taken this precaution.

3. When going off on a hike, take protective clothing. You may get caught in the rain. A light rain jacket is easy to carry and will help to protect you from discomfort. Take a bit of food with you. That chocolate bar or fruit will sustain you when you get tired and will be invaluable if you get lost and are out on the trail longer than you expected to be.

4. Take a compass and map. Don't rely on your instincts or intuition. The woods have a way of fooling the unwary and uncautious. If you must leave a trail, blaze your way on trees or use rocks or sticks so you can find your way back again.

5. Arrange a signal with your fellow hikers to be used when you get lost. Use it for emergency only and stay put while you signal so the rescuers can come to you more readily.

6. If one hiker has a serious accident, make him as comfortable as possible and leave him on the trail with someone to stand guard and then go for help. Do not try to carry him back. You may do more harm than good.

Available State and Federal Public Camping Grounds

New camping grounds are being built and existing ones improved all over the country. For the latest information about such areas write:

United States Department of Agriculture, Forest Service. Ask for the booklet *National Park Vacations.*

This will give locations of camping areas in every state in the union as well as Alaska and Puerto Rico. It includes information about facilities for picnicking and camping, winter sports, hunting and fishing, auto roads and hiking trails. A map will be included to help you plot your camping expedition. Also available from the United States Government are:

The National Park System (Eastern United States)
Camping Facilities in the National Park System
The National Park System (Western United States)
National Parks (Historic Sites—National Monuments)
Also available are:

1. *How to See America Now,* a guide to vacation fun in National and State Parks;

2. A recreational map of the United States.

Both are published by *This Week* Magazine, P.O. Box 239, Radio City Station, New York 19, N.Y.

3. *The Handbook of Auto Camping and Motorist's Guide to Public Campgrounds* by George and Iris Wells. Published by Harper & Brothers, New York.

Picnic Basket

On camping trips, the picnic basket is an invaluable part of camping equipment. En route it will come in handy as you stop at wayside tables for lunch. It will eliminate the necessity of doing a major job of unpacking for each meal. At camp it will be invaluable when you leave the camp site to explore and expect to be away at lunchtime. See chapter on family picnics for equipment which goes into the basket.

Chic Sale Department

Needed: Shovel and imagination, short ropes, two-by-fours, stout wooden boxes, ax, knife, maybe even an umbrella, canvas, bag of lime, wood ashes.

Whatever you call it—head, john, toilet—this is a necessary and vital part of any camp where such facilities are not otherwise available.

1. If you are in a grove of trees standing close together and you are going to be in camp for quite a while, try this one. Dig a hole at the base of three or more handy trees. Cut yourself some stout branches and lash them at whatever height you wish in a triangle above the hole, using trees to lash to. You may then assure privacy

by weaving branches or stretching a small tarpaulin around two sides of your triangle of trees.

Do not neglect to use the extra dirt accumulated by your effort in digging the hole, the lime or, in absence of lime, the wood ashes. Either is shoveled into the hole after each usage thus eliminating unpleasant appearance and odor.

2. Simplest construction is a stout wooden box set on a couple of logs and poised over a hole. Don't try to use fruit crates—they are liable to give way and precipitate you downward. This is not good. A lean-to of canvas or an umbrella lashed above will comfort you in the rain.

3. Probably the most successful of all toilets is created beside a fast-flowing stream of surface water. If the stream empties into a river already polluted you need have no qualms about further contaminating the stream. Nail a stout wooden box on two two-by-fours, knock a hole in the box and set the two-by-fours across the stream from bank to bank. Over the whole contraption, hang an umbrella. Toilet paper should be placed conveniently near by but kept in a covered tin can. This protects it from the weather and from mice who love to burrow inside paper.

Camp Cookery on Tin Can Stoves

Camp cookery is an imaginative art learned as a rule by trial and error. Since there are many books on this subject, this type of experimentation is unnecessary. One incorrect assumption is that the adults are the only ones involved in this gentle art. Children can be taught to cook satisfactory and leisurely meals out of doors. As a matter of fact, the techniques of out-of-doors cooking are easily transferable indoors. If Mother can stand the confusion, she might find it advantageous to control her housewifely instincts long enough to have an hour's extra sleep while Junior happily gets breakfast, practicing techniques learned over a campfire.

Expensive camp cookery outfits are not the only prerequisite of good food. You can make cook stoves out of tin cans. Two-pound coffee cans or cans measuring five or six inches high and the same in diameter will be satisfactory. Take the lid off, reverse the can so that the open end is on the ground. Now cut an opening about four by four inches on one side of the can at the bottom edge. Opposite the door in the back of the can and near the top, cut an opening to let the smoke out. Don't disturb the cooking area (formerly the bottom of the can) which has a convenient rim around it to retain the grease or cooking fat. Your stove is now ready for use. You can build your small fire first and set the can on top of it or you may prefer to feed paper and small twigs into the opening. Be careful. Your stove heats up in a hurry. If the opening faces the wind you will be spared the trial of upending yourself to blow in the door.

A row of tin cans will cook a variety of foods. If you time it right everything will finish cooking at the same time. The coffee pot or the teapot should be started first. Once the water is boiling, if you have vegetables to cook, you do those next. The meat is the last to be started.

Bacon and eggs, hamburgers, lamb chops, steaks taste wonderful when cooked on a tin can stove. Best of all, each person may cook his own. This is how Junior learns his camp cookery. He finds that it is not necessary to have a large fire or a great amount of wood. He learns the order in which food is cooked so that it all comes out ready to eat at the same time. He learns what *not* to do in order that his hamburger is neither raw nor overcooked. Perhaps better than any knowledge gained, he acquires a healthy respect for his mother's ability to put a good and nourishing meal on the table. Best of all since no one likes to wash out fry pans, tin can stoves can be thrown away after using. A new stove is available as long as the supply of tin cans lasts.

Skunks

If you have never been a string saver, start the habit before you go camping. That small piece of ordinary cotton grocery store string may come in handy in case you are invaded by a family of skunks or even *one* skunk. That usually mild and harmless animal can, if he wishes, rout you out of camp faster than a tornado. While you are weeping and coughing remember where the string is. Tie one end of the string to a branch or rafter or nail above your head and light the hanging end. It will smolder and in no time at all the skunk smell will be gone. The string need not be very long—three feet or less—and you may wish to hang several pieces in several places.

If your dog goes charging out and comes back with his tail at half-mast, his ears drooping and the "wot happened" look in his eye, do not disinherit him. Hold your nose and open a can of tomatoes or tomato juice and douse his coat and rub it in. Both you and he will be happy after you have washed the tomatoes out of his fur.

6

Hobbies and Family Fun

The word "hobby" has been used too often to apply only to that type of activity in which people make something with their hands or gather things together in collections. Often the activities so termed have been of such low quality that the word has come into ill repute and many turn up their noses at the mention of it and snort derisively: "Huh, hobbies, they're for children."

Webster defines a hobby as a favored pursuit, which would make the choice of activities practically limitless. The experienced hobbyist smiles at this definition and questions which is the pursuer and which the pursued. Many a hobbyist has one time or another suddenly found himself holding a wild thing by the tail or asked himself by what wild thing he has been seized, so violent can the reaction be when a new interest taken up suddenly takes over.

Hobbies actually cover more than the categories of making or collecting things. They include doing things and learning things as well. Seldom does any hobbyist begin in one category and remain there. The pursuit of one interest may lead him from one area into another without his realizing it. This is particularly true when the hobby lies within the realm of creative activity.

There is no question that some activities termed hobbies are a waste of time and money. They tend to clutter people's minds with useless information and their homes with unsightly junk. While they may do no harm they do no good either. Their worst offense is that they give a poor return on the individual's investment of time which is his most priceless possession.

Some hobbies satisfy man's desire to *learn* more about himself and the world in which he lives. This leads to the pursuit of such activities as reading, studying, experimenting and exploring. Some fill man's need to create with his hands so he turns to these activities in which he *makes* or builds things, such as furniture, art objects or a stone garden wall. The *doing* hobbies satisfy the individuals who are happiest when engaged in sports or games or in performing services which are beneficial to others. The *collecting* hobbies are most attractive to those who find happiness and satisfaction in bringing like things together in one place.

Whether the hobbyist pursues a doing, making, learning or collecting hobby is not so important as whether the interest has all the attributes of the truly creative activity. Such a hobby fosters growth because the individual can grow with the hobby rather than outgrow it. Through the pursuit of his interest he develops useful skills, acquires valuable knowledge and gains in wisdom and understanding. Fluidity is characteristic of the relationship between the hobbyist and his interest. The situation is rarely static. There is always some new goal to reach for, something new to learn, some degree of skill still to achieve.

People may be born with talents and aptitudes. Through early training in good homes, these talents are brought to light and given opportunity to develop. The talents may be inborn but the skills which utilize them must be acquired. How these skills are used in later years is often influenced by early home training. The child who has been read to from carefully selected books will not be satisfied with junk literature after he learns to read for himself. The boy who is a natural born collector can be encouraged to collect stamps instead of useless bits of junk. Stamp collecting involves more than the accumulating of miscellaneous bits of perforated gummed paper. A good collection necessitates a knowledge of geography, history and foreign currency as well as information about current issues and their catalogue values.

Beginning a hobby is like the first move in a chess game. At first there are only a few possibilities but with each subsequent move the combinations increase a hundredfold. To illustrate, take a beginner

in the art of metal jewelry making. He can work in silver, copper or gold, with flat metal or with wire. Wire can be drawn into flat, round, half-round or square shapes. It can be made up in beaded forms of all sizes. It can be fashioned into links or a dozen designs. Two or more strands of the same or varying thickness can be twisted together to form bracelets or as embellishments for rings, pendants or pins. Different metals can be used together for interesting contrasts.

In designing his pieces, the hobbyist becomes acquainted with jewelry designed by the craftsman of China, the Near East, the Mexican and American Indian. He learns to distinguish between the work of the Zuni Indians and the Navahos. He will not confuse the jewelry of the Egyptian with that of the Thai.

He will study the designs of the ancient as well as the modern jewelry maker. When he makes his own pieces they may show the influence of one type or another but his designs will be his own.

In the process of making jewelry he will become acquainted with all manner of semiprecious or precious stones. He will learn by study or bitter experience which are hard and which are soft and easily cracked or chipped. He will learn about intaglios and cameos. He will soon be able to tell the genuine stone from the clever imitations of glass or plastic.

If he travels to regions where gem material is found in its natural state, he will trudge miles, climb hills, and dig up vast areas until he triumphantly comes up with a "find." The energies of rock hounds are nigh inexhaustible and their tongues are worn smooth from licking stones to see how they will look when polished.

The hobbyist may then go on to polishing his own sets and add the art of the lapidary to his skills. The hobby he has pursued literally pushed him into a variety of activities challenging him with questions to answer, problems to be solved and obstacles to overcome. If he responds to the challenges he will acquire a liberal education in geography, history, metallurgy, modern and ancient arts and crafts and geology. He will have developed patience, self-discipline, perserverance and his powers of observation as well as skills in one or more allied subects. His horizons have been pushed back time and time again.

This is only part of what happens to the hobbyist. In his enthusiasm he cannot keep such a good thing to himself. He has to tell others about it. He is abubble with the good news. His enthusiasm wins converts and he draws some of his friends or family into the charmed circle. He seeks out others who are experimenting. He enrolls in classes to increase his proficiency. He joins a club of gem collectors or lapidaries. He swaps his duplicates for those of other collectors. His creations become numerous. He supplies his friends and family members with gifts he has made and still has a surplus. With encouragement he exhibits in arts and craft shows. He may even find a market for his work.

All or any of these things can happen. Added to these benefits is the joy of hours of actual creation, the deep pleasure of working with hands and tools and the complete satisfaction that comes when a plan has been conceived and carried through to conclusion. The mind has been stimulated, the creative urge has been satisfied, the circle of friends has been enlarged and strengthened and there has been a liberal education. All this has been accomplished in hours filled with soul-satisfying fun.

The collecting hobbyists gather bits of this and that together. At first glance their collections seem to be of little value until we take a closer look. Much of the history of man has been ferreted out and preserved by these collectors with their seemingly innocent and unimportant pastimes. Natural history, historical and art museums are monuments to individuals and groups of individuals with similar interests who have banded together in order to bring together collections of all kinds that are of immeasurable worth in the search for knowledge about man's activities since his earliest beginnings.

Whether we call these collectors archaeologists, philatelists, numismatists, naturalists, antique collectors or rock hounds, these amateurs in many fields of endeavors have made untold contributions to man's knowledge about the beginnings of life, his world and the universe of which his world is a part.

While it takes a trained mind to gather all these bits of evidence together to determine their worth and meaning, in the beginning it is the amateur who collects a large portion of them. The more observant the amateur, the more he recognizes the value of his findings even though he may not always be able to grasp their full significance.

One thing a hobby definitely does is to develop one's powers of observation and it thereby serves a valuable purpose in the life of the hobbyist. For a man must *see* a thing before he can put it to his use. Many of us have "eyes that see not and ears that hear not." It is this power to see and observe that distinguishes the alert organism from a vegetative blob of existence. All of man's progress is attributable to man's ability to *see* bits of evidence which he can gather together and toss into the great melting pot of progress.

Consider the many great men and women who have sought out painstakingly, one by one, the facts that have resulted in the discoveries of some of the great truths which have enabled man to triumph over ignorance and superstition. These scientists, explorers, writers, philosophers and leaders have struggled onward, driven by some inner force with little or no thought of monetary gain or personal recognition. (That these may have come afterward does not detract from the fact that it was the drive for knowledge which motivated them.) But no discovery, no invention, no great movement is the product of one man's efforts. The efforts and contributions of many lives have gone into their making—the efforts of many little people—the amateurs. The skills of the professional and amateur may be comparable, but the amateur chooses not to make his living by means of this particular skill. In other fields, the difference between the amateur and the professional hinges not only upon whether he gets paid for his efforts but upon the extent of his professional training.

But whatever his skill and whether or not it is important to his livelihood, it is not one with which he was born. He acquired it and developed it. This is true of the amateurs in other fields who are *making* things or *collecting* things or *learning* about things. In this latter group many important contributions have been made to man's fund of knowledge by the amateurs, the professionally untrained seekers of knowledge. Amateur astronomers, many of whom started out by making telescopes (another example of how a hobby carries one from one field of endeavor to another), have watched the skies with almost fanatic faithfulness and have discovered many novae (new stars) overlooked by the professional astronomers too busy with other matters.

Great strides in the development of radio were made by the scientifically untrained "hams" who in spite of their lack of professional training often accomplished the impossible because they didn't know that such things could not be done. Public acclaim has been given these amateurs who maintain a network of communications around the world and perform invaluable services in times of crises and need.

The voyage of the *Kon-Tiki* came as a result of an experiment of six men, skilled in other fields, but amateurs in the navigation of a raft. By accomplishing what most professionals thought was a foolhardy impossibility they added another link to man's chain of knowledge.

The reform movements, the great humanitarian experiments, have been carried on and given life by the people whose hobbies were not *making, collecting* or *learning* but in *doing* things. By their efforts these amateurs in the field of human relations give strength and impetus to the Boy Scout, Girl Scout and Camp Fire Girl movements. They keep alive the Red Cross, the Parent-Teacher Associations, the National Conference of Christians and Jews, The Consumers' League and all institutions dedicated to human betterment.

While we may credit the beginnings of these great movements to one or two inspired leaders, without the devoted support of the hundreds and thousands of amateurs—the volunteers, the lay boards, the committees, the active members, the inactive but financially supporting members—who by virtue of their numbers give strength and continuity to these movements, they might have died abirthing.

The world is a better place because of these persons who devote a part of their leisure to performing labors of love for the betterment of humanity with no thought of personal or financial gain. As the craftsmen labor to create beautiful things and the musicians beautiful music, these hobbyists labor to create a happier world. They satisfy their drive to create in the advancement of human relations, in the betterment of working conditions and in the improvement of their schools and government.

What we call the pursuits of the *makers,* the *collectors,* the *learners* and the *doers* is of little importance. Call them hobbies, vital activities, avocations or outside interests or whatever. What is important is that these individuals have put their leisure time to creative use. They have given meaning to their lives in their wise use of their free hours. They have given dignity and value to their leisure hours often far surpassing that of their work lives which may have served as a means of financial support, but have contributed little to the development of their personalities and the betterment of their communities.

Family members of all ages can follow hobbies together. Many have no limit on age range. The stamp collector father and collector son can spend hours together working at their hobby together. The stamp club they join can be the same as most clubs are open to philatelists of all ages. Handicap sports such as bowling or golf are good father-son or mother-daughter activities. Neither holds the other back since each competes only against his own score. Swimming, skating and other such sports are good family activities. We have already discussed crafts and arts as family hobby activities. And so far as collectors are concerned, age is no problem. If two collectors have the same interest, no one asks the age of the other before making a swap.

There remains much to be done in the world. There are vitally important bits of evidence to be collected, items of beauty to be gathered together, examples of culture to be preserved, Old World skills to be learned and perpetuated. A goodly portion of this work must be done by the amateurs in their hours of play. Leisure is one of man's most precious assets. How he uses this time will determine its worth and value. He can use it to improve his civilization or destroy it. Early and determined home training has much to do with his decision. Hobbies are an important part of his training. Parents who share their creative interests with their children are opening doors to fascinating worlds of beauty, adventure and service.

7

Fun with Family Home Industries

In these days of fancy frozen, canned, dried and otherwise processed foods there seems no good reason for families to engage in canning, preserving or baking activities unless they have large gardens and need to preserve the surpluses they cannot sell, eat or give away. Home canning, however, can be an enjoyable family activity if it is done at a time when most of the family is at home and can participate.

Collect the family sometime and turn them loose with a bushel of peaches to be prepared for canning. Everybody from three years up can join the fun. Somebody prepares the containers or jars. Some sit around the preparation table and peel the fruit. Quite a lot of sampling goes on just to be sure the fruit is good enough to can. One member races with another to see which can peel a peach faster. The air is filled with the fragrant scent of the fruit and the voices of the workers vying with each other. When the job is done and the cleaning-up process completed, the row of jars or containers brings an immense feeling of satisfaction. But the best of the job is yet to come in the eating. Weeks later the whole family will literally enjoy the fruits of their labors and remember all over again with each succulent bite how much fun they had. There will come a time when someone wishes to make a gift to a friend. A container of the home-preserved fruit will be a most welcome one, appreciated not only for its tasty goodness but for the fact that it is the product of the giver's own labors.

Families have their own special recipes which have been handed down from generation to generation. Certain jellies and jams, pickles or preserves made in the home kitchen as family projects become truly home industries. Families can hand-print or have printed their own special labels which may give an interesting explanation as well as the name of the delicacy in the container. If they are asked to do so by the grateful recipients of these special foods, they may even give out the recipe.

The pride a family takes in making some of its own special foods makes for strong family feelings. The preparation of these foods annually becomes an important family tradition. The friends who receive containers of these family specialties look forward to these gifts with an eager anticipation which is very satisfying to the givers.

The making of Christmas candy or special cookies is also a tradition in some families. Hours and hours are spent in preparing pounds of special cookies and candies as gifts to friends. Each year these

families try to find unusual containers or different ways of packaging the goodies to enhance their gifts.

Some families bake traditional pastries according to some Old

World recipes and give these as holiday gifts to their friends. Others find that just baking homemade bread and surprising their friends any day of the year is a good family home industry activity.

Through this medium, the children learn valuable homemaking skills while enjoying all the fun of family togetherness. Added to the joy of doing something together as a family there is the enjoyment of giving some away to delighted and surprised friends and, last but not least, the fun of eating the products themselves.

No special equipment is required for family home industries. The same utensils used for family cooking and baking are used. The trick is to get the whole family into the act. From the smallest to the biggest a job must be found. There are nuts to crack and pick over, raisins to clean, pans to grease, dishes to wash, cookies to decorate, packages to wrap, flour to sift, ingredients to measure, eggs to beat and pans to lick. Everybody does the job or jobs suited to his age and experience. No special recipes are necessary—just use ones your family have found to be favorites.

Special jars of attractive shapes are saved for gift jars for pickles, preserves or jellies. Unusual wrappings make the gifts more attractive. Labels or gift enclosures are used so that the whole family gets credit for the gift. Some suggested projects for family home industries are listed below:

1. Baking and decorating birthday cakes for friends and relatives
2. Baking special pies for surprise gifts
3. Jellies and jams in odd and unusual jars or wrapped in unusual ways for gifts
4. Homemade candies of one type or several specially packaged and wrapped
5. Special jars of pickles or preserves attractively put up and wrapped
6. Christmas cookies of many varieties nicely packaged
7. Christmas cookies suitably decorated to be used as Christmas tree ornaments or table decorations
8. Special breads or coffee rings attractively decorated and boxed

All family industries need not center around food. See also the chapter on family crafts which gives directions for Christmas candles and decorations, May baskets, Christmas tree decorations, etc. which are suitable for gifts and are made by the whole family.

Gifts that are made with loving care with certain friends in mind are fun to make and mean much, much more to the recipients when they know the circumstances under which the gifts were made. The products of our hearts and hands carry with them some of the warmth of family feeling that was generated during the process of creating them. The joy of creating makes the best flavoring.

8

Music in Family Living

The need for music is universal. No one realizes this more clearly than those who have been raised on music and to whom the idea of being without it is unthinkable. If we are sad, we find comfort in music. If we are happy, it gives wings to our joy. It relaxes us when we are tired and soothes us when we are distressed. If we are confused it helps to orient us and it has a healing quality when we are sick.

Music has been a part of man's life since his earliest beginnings. Throughout the ages it has been a means and an end in his neverending search for beauty. He used its rhythmic sounds to express his every emotion. He used music in every phase of living. He developed music with which to talk to and entreat his gods. Some of his songs told of his love of country, home or family. If courting he furthered his cause with a wistful love song or a haunting melody played on a flute. To make his work easier, he chanted rhythmically because music produced the effect needed to achieve the strength of unison for heavy lifting and pushing. He used music to promote the unity of spirit at large gatherings, to incite groups to war, create peaceful harmony or to strengthen an appeal to the gods for rain or bountiful harvest. Primitive tribes today still employ these methods.

We, the so-called civilized creatures, still need music. While our mode of living is different, basically we are very little different from early man in our needs, urges and drives. We still need to express our emotions by satisfying means; we still need to talk to our God; we need the means to create beauty through the medium of sound and rhythm.

If our instruments now are more complicated and our music more complex, the music fills the same needs as it has for ages past. Music lifts our spirits, reduces tensions, expresses our joys and sorrows, sets the rhythms for our dances, soothes and comforts the fretful and

makes our work easier and less fatiguing. Like early man, we have our religious chants and hymns, national anthems, love songs, lullabies, work songs, dance music, drinking and nonsense songs.

Music dissolves racial and national barriers. It wipes out the differences of age or social status. It is the universal language understood by all. It is the language of love and understanding uniting all peoples.

Music can be an individual or group experience. When we join with others in singing and the harmonies are sweet and true, our spirits rise as if on wings and our hearts seem to fill our chests and push against our ribs and make us wish the song fest would never end. If the singers are of all ages and are family groups as they are at some church conferences, the universal power of music again makes itself felt. When people of all ages and backgrounds can raise their voices together in unison or melodious harmonies, something happens to the group and to each individual. Harmony of thought and unification of purpose is achieved to a degree it could not otherwise be.

Music has its lessons and its disciplines. The better we wish our music to be, the greater our skills must be. We learn that hours of practice must precede each minor achievement but the rewards far outweigh the hours of toil. When we sing in a chorus or play in an orchestra, we find that teamwork and the subjugation of the individual to the good of the whole is as important here as it is on the athletic field. We learn, too, that the thrill of being a part of the whole overshadows any sacrifice of individuality that is required of us.

As we build up experience upon musical experience, each familiar melody recalls a pleasant memory. Families who make a practice of singing together before the fireside, around the picnic campfire or around the Christmas tree build the foundations for a lifetime of happy memories. The sounds of the familiar carols at Christmastime will recall for the singer the happy hours of Christmas at home in years past. The familiar strains of a lullaby will recall the time when Mother sat at the bedside of the child fretful with the discomforts of measles or some childhood disease.

It is indeed a rare individual who does not respond to music. Musical talent need not be of concert stage quality to bring pleasure to singer or instrumentalist. Some families have their own little orchestras composed of piano or accordion, a bass fiddle gut-bucket made of washtub and washline, harmonica or whatever instrument Junior or Sister happens to be studying at the time. The sounds coming forth may not be exactly pleasing to the neighbors but they sound mighty sweet and give much joyful satisfaction to the players.

Experiences such as these are within the reach of any who count music as an important part of their lives. Whenever people raise their voices in song together, or two or more instrumentalists get together for a session, the potentialities for soul-stirring joys are there. Whether the music is made by as simple an instrument as a shepherd's pipe or harmonica or one as complicated as a piano or a clarinet, if the music comes from the heart, all the potentials are there. Whatever the song, if sung with whole heart, our troubles melt and our spirits soar. "Lift up your hearts and sing," say the words of a song. Live with music and it will give you new life.

Radio and record players have brought good music performed by fine artists and orchestras into our homes but no musical culture can steadily grow or long endure if the people spend all their time listening to and no time in making music. Children must be taught to sing and to play instruments. Music must be an active as well as passive part of their lives. Every skilled musician and every composer must have his early beginnings. His talent does not suddenly burst into blossom. There must be time for planting and a time for growing before there can be a tuneful harvest.

No family leisure program is complete without music. It reaches into every corner of our lives, brightening the dark ones, intensifying the bright. Our ability to fit music into our pattern of life, like other acquired abilities, must be nurtured. We must train our minds and bodies to understand and respond to music so that we may derive the full benefits of its wondrous and life-enriching powers.

Imagine a church service without the singing of the congregational hymns, a school rally without the alma mater or Christmas without carols and you have a fair picture of family life without music as an integral part. Families who make music a part of their lives need no sales talk. Those who do not, miss one of the great joys of family living.

In most school systems, boys and girls have the opportunity of singing in school choirs and playing in school orchestras or bands. Some participate in these activities all through junior and senior high school and if they go on to college join such organizations there. Once they are out of school, very often these opportunities cease and all this trained musical talent is allowed to go to waste. Many communities now, however, are realizing that such talent can be used to advantage long after the school years are over. Choruses, community bands and orchestras are springing up all over the country giving opportunity for these musical amateurs to continue enjoying the fun of participation all their lives. Most of these organizations are open to persons of all ages. Thus parents and children can join these groups and participate together as family units enjoying the chance to sing or play music they could not perform at home with only a few persons.

If your community offers no such opportunities contact your recreation department or school board. You may be surprised how much interest is evidenced and how much talent is anxious for a chance to be heard once the opportunity presents itself.

9

Family Fun with Nature Activities

Some adventures in recreational activities lift our hearts, stimulate our minds, make new friends for us or challenge our manual dexterity, but more than in any other of the leisure time activities experience with Nature teaches us humbleness. We have only to stand quietly under the stars to realize our smallness. We need only a thoughtful walk through the woods to understand the insignificance and yet vital importance of each tiny part of life that makes up the whole.

Primitive man was much aware of the forces and wonders of Nature which surrounded him. With his musical instruments he attempted to imitate the sounds he heard. His flute sang the songs of the wind and the birds. Some of his dance movements were patterned after the swaying motions of the trees and tall grasses. Thunder was in his drums. He observed the animals and birds and made their motions his dance movements. He took the colors from plants and used them to brighten his clothing, tools, weapons and dwelling. He and Nature had a oneness. He was a child of Nature.

We are no less children of Nature today but we sometimes lose sight of the fact, surrounded as we are with man-made things. We tend to forget our close relationship with Nature until she sends us a terrible reminder in one of her mad moments. She tears the roof off our house with a mighty wind; destroys the tender buds on our trees and shrubs with a killing frost; paralyzes our city with a blanket of snow; or splits the trunk of our shade tree with a bolt of lightning.

Then we remember that in spite of our modern ways, we are still basically and fundamentally Nature's children dependent upon her for all the necessities of life—indeed, for life itself. Her reminders may not always be starkly dramatic. They may be gentle, vividly

beautiful, deliciously fragrant or filled with breath-taking majesty. If we take the time to appreciate her wonders, we grow quiet within. We are comforted by the thought that all of this beauty is a part of us as we are a part of it.

A child even when very young is conscious of the wonders around him. He needs nothing to stimulate his awareness, for such is the quality of childhood that everything new and strange is filled with wonder. At first he needs only answers to his questions which despite his tender years can be real posers! "Why is the sky blue? What is snow? Who put these pictures on the window? Is the moon broken? Where does the wind go?"

Later the encouragement fostered by his parents' interest and observations will not only keep his questioning mind active, but will stimulate him to seek out the answers by careful observation or from books.

We are by nature sensuous. The things that gratify our senses have strong appeal for us. Nature has the means to gratify all our senses. For our taste pleasures her storehouses provide us with foods that are bitter, salty or spicy or sweet, that are chewy, juicy, soft, prickly, mushy, stringy, meaty or crisp. She gives us foods that nourish and sustain life. She has her store of poisons that can make us uncomfortable and at worst can kill us. Her medicine cabinet is filled with roots, herbs, blossoms, fruits, seeds and molds that relieve symptoms, cure illnesses and restore men and animals to health.

"Taste of Nature" Game

The family on a nature walk can play a taste game sampling leaves or fruits of the plants that grow along the path. The leaf of the wintergreen will taste like teaberry gum. The oxalis or sour grass will leave an acidy, lemony taste in the mouth. The milky substance in a dandelion stem will pucker the mouth with its gall-like bitterness. How good the raspberries and blackberries are! How pungently fresh is the leaf of the mint. The tenderfoot will never more than once taste the jack-in-the-pulpit root (Indian turnip) raw again. His tongue and throat will feel as if he had bitten into a pincushion and swallowed it whole.

Danger—There's Poison in Those Woods

The youthful nature enthusiast should be taught to recognize and avoid poison ivy and poison oak and to know how to treat himself if he has been exposed to it. A careful washing of possibly exposed parts with strong brown soap is always a good precautionary measure after a walk in the woods. Even the most careful hiker can walk through a patch of poison ivy or have it brush against his bare legs or arms before he realizes it. Washing will help to prevent the poisoning effect. Commercially prepared lotions and cures are sold in every drugstore. Jewelweed can be gathered and the sap from the stems rubbed on exposed areas. The leaves, stems and blossoms of jewelweed if cooked chopped until they resemble a pot of spinach will bring relief when applied to ivy-poisoned spots on the body. This mixture can be kept in a jar in the refrigerator and will stay effective for many weeks.

Mushrooms, which are so good if edible and so bad if poisonous, should not be eaten unless you are absolutely certain of the variety. While tasting is fun, be sure of the plant before you chew or eat. Do not sample indiscriminately. This applies to berries as well.

"Listen to Nature" Game

The sounds of Nature are always around us. It is fun just to sit quietly in one spot and selectively begin to identify the various sounds we hear. Unless the day is exceedingly still, the wind will be heard rustling through the leaves, crying or howling around corners of buildings. Water makes different sounds depending on its location. Waves will roar as they fling themselves against the rocks and shore. Water racing over hidden rocks in a swiftly moving stream will make rumbling, rippling sounds or sucking sounds as it pulls away from irregular banks and twists into eddies.

Birds will have different sounds when they are awakening in the morning than when they are sleepily settling themselves for the night. They have their mating songs, their scolding-the-cat or admonishing-their-young sounds and their chattering-over-dinner voices.

Animal sounds are a veritable symphony. The high notes in the score are played by the squeaking, squealing rodents. The bullfrog plays the bass pizzicato style. Some make the sustained tones, roaring, bleating, neighing, hee-hawing and mooing. Others contribute the short staccato notes by chattering and barking. The beaver thumps his tail and plays the bass drum. The squirrels and chipmunks chatter like a roll on a snare drum.

We do not need to be in the woods to play the nature listening game. We can lie in our beds at home and listen to the rain pounding at our windows or dripping from the eaves on the ground below. We cannot close our ears to the crash of thunder. The wind has a way of shaking the house, rattling the window, whistling under the door.

To a child trained to use his ears in this manner, these are friendly sounds. They challenge him to a guessing contest. Is the rain propelled against the windows in large blots or fine misty spray? Hear that thunder? Wait for the next flash of lightning and begin to count. Count slowly as "one and a thousand, two and a thousand." Count until you hear the thunder. Since light travels faster than sound, you will see the lightning before you hear the thunder. Each number tolled off represents a mile. Count to five—the storm is five miles away. Is it coming closer or moving away? Wait for the next flash, count again. Six counts this time. Now it is seven. Ah! the storm is moving away. To such a child, the storm is not a fearful visitation of nature to hide from under the bed but a natural phenomenon which brings rain to nourish the crops and make the grass green again. A parent has but to play such a game with his child a time or two and it becomes the child's. Knowledge helps him to combat fears.

Storms can have their fanciful folklore explanations as well as their natural ones. A parent explains that thunder is the little men playing at their bowling game. The alley lights up for a moment, the little man bowls his ball. A loud crash means he has hit the pins squarely and made a strike. See. They've turned on the lights again. Wait a moment, he's bowling now. Wham! another strike. The imaginative mind of the child takes over. Fear of the storm turns into a make-believe game, awesome still but no longer frightening.

"Nature and Our Noses" Game

Sometimes we can concentrate on smells when we take a nature walk in the woods. In the woods our noses are challenged at almost every step. Say! What smells so sweet? Aha! It's the mandrake (May apple) in bloom over there! Crush this leaf. Savory and pungent like an herb, isn't it? Phew! Must be a skunk around here! Break a pine needle in your fingers. Isn't it fresh and aromatic? Shuffle your feet in these dry leaves. Don't they give off a dusty, nose-tickling smell? Turn over these wet leaves here. Musty, moldy odor, isn't it?

Even on drives we can play the smelling game. Shut your eyes and keep them closed. (Not the driver, of course. He's the referee!)

What's that funny odor? Must be cabbages. Smells like sewer gas. Hey! who opened the cologne bottle? That's a field of white clover. That smell? You can't fool us on that one! Nothing smells like that but new-mown hay. Oh, boy! Grapes ripening in the sun! Phew, we just passed a beach. Dead fish washed up on the shore.

Each plant, each place, each season has its own peculiar brand of scent. The trillium is reminiscent of gardenia, so heavy is its fragrance. Woodland smells can never be mistaken for those of open and cultivated fields or those of marsh and bog. Spring's scent is a delicate cologne, new and fresh; summer's is a perfume, rich and penetrating; fall's is a fragrant, haunting incense; winter's is an ointment, its indefinable fragrances dulled by the cold. All are part of Nature's potpourri for our delight, free for the taking.

The "Touch Me" Game

The exploring finger of a baby is a delightful thing to watch. It pokes here, touches there, probes and pinches. He learns much about his environment with this sensitive instrument. As he grows older he becomes aware of many sensations transmitted through other parts of his body. Play a game as you drive along sometime, listing the many different feels Nature has. Then when the opportunity presents itself, test these varieties for yourself. How soft is the velvet of the gloxinia petal! How feathery some dry grasses are! Rub your fingers over the petals of the bristly strawflower. Feel the filelike edge of the whiskers of ripe wheat or the softness of a young kitten or puppy. Is there anything downier than a young chick? Let the warm sand run through your fingers and warm dust push up through your toes as you walk barefooted. Rub your hand along the abrasive surface of that granite boulder. Hold a smooth quartz pebble in your palm. How warm the summer rain feels against your face. Not so long ago snow needles used your face for a pincushion. Moss is a spongy resilient carpet; lichens are flaky and dry under our feet. Remember when the mud played tug-o'-war with your rubbers and won? How squeaky the snow is on a near-zero day! Recall the time the slush crawled in over your overshoe top and wormed its way into your shoe? Ugh! Brush

that cobweb off my face. Help, get me loose from that brier. Aah!
the sun is burning a hole in my back! Oooh! King Winter just ran
an icy finger down my spine! Whoops, watch your footing here!
There's nothing slipperier than an algae-covered rock. Wade over
here to this shallow pool. Warm, isn't it? Nature's own little foot
bath. Hey! This mountain stream is cold. Who emptied the ice cube
tray in it? Gosh, that's a sharp wind. Phew! isn't it muggy today?
Ouch! That branch just slapped my face. Hey, who pinched me? If
you weren't a thistle, I'd pinch you back!

So it goes, hot, cold, dry, wet, smooth, rough, slimy, velvety. No
end of things to feel. Some are pleasant, some repulsive. The varieties
are endless. There is something to challenge us at every turn. It is
impossible to be indifferent or bored.

Nature's Art Gallery

To gratify our sense of sight, Nature has turned her hand in every
direction and left nothing untouched to delight our eyes. Look! Perfection of design is everywhere—in the spiral of a snail shell, the
veining of a leaf, in the heart of a tulip. Examine the design in the
cross-section of a carrot or the flowing line of the willow. Marvel at
the never duplicated geometric patterns of the snowflakes. Nature's
objets d'art are to be found in our refrigerator, in our own back yard,
in the park or forest reserve.

Look for the original scenes from which man has taken his ideas.
Like a charcoal study? Black trees outlined with snow placed against
a winter's gray sky are one of winter's breath-taking sights. A summer
pastoral? See the cattle standing sleepily under the protecting shade
of a stately elm in the shimmering heat of an August afternoon.
Snow-capped mountains against the sky, jewel-toned waters blending
with the sky are Nature's land- and seascapes.

Nature's Whimseys

Nature has her bag of tricks and jokes and provides us with oddi-
ties, both humorous and beautiful. She has put eyes in the tail of the
peacock and painted floral designs with frost on our windows. With

her mirages she fools us into seeing things that aren't there at all. Playing magician she gives animals and birds protective coloring so that they can disappear before our eyes. Clouds are bowls of mashed potatoes; some animals have four eyes, two to see with and two to confuse us. Venus is a brilliant diamond in the evening sky; a dewdrop is an opal for a few minutes in the morning sun. With one sweep of her brush Nature blends all her colors into a rainbow. A monkey looks like a human; a human has the doleful look of a bloodhound. Two people totally unrelated look enough alike to be twins, and two brothers are totally different.

Some insects eat plants and there are plants that eat insects. Nature has given us sights to tickle our fancies. She challenges our power of observation and provides us with flashes of beauty or sights so terrible they chill our spines.

Nature in Motion

Not only has Nature given us color and design, but she has put them in motion. Play a what-does-it-look-like game as you observe motion in nature. Watch a titmouse in flight. He rides a wind roller coaster as he flies. See! The wind is pushing the clouds across the skies. Ah, the breeze just nudged the grass into motion. Look at the acres of tulips dancing to the tune of the wind. Now they're bowing and curtsying in stately minuet; now their motion is that of a hootchy-kootchy dancer. The dead leaves are riding wind elevators; the hawk hangs on an invisible string.

Something is always in motion, upward, downward, across our line of vision, toward us, away from us, moving slowly, swiftly, gracefully or clumsily. Nature, the master choreographer, has blended the motions in one tremendous production to which the admission is but an observing, appreciate pair of eyes.

What! You say the arts don't interest you? Music, motion, design, color—these are for the artist. You're more the mechanical type—the engineering aspects of things are your meat. Good! Take a good look at a garter snake. Most wonderful piece of engineering in the world. Watch a hawk in flight. Man has a long way to go to build that kind of glider! How about a dandelion? Now there is a wonderful little machine. Pull one apart petal by petal, leaf by leaf. Engineered to perfection, is it not?

Musician, artist, dancer, designer, engineer, teacher, preacher, whatever you are, Nature can teach you a few things about your field. Her store of facts is limitless. The regularity of night and day, season following season, the movement of the stars—all are comforting and wonderful. But Nature can be as inconsistent as she is consistent. Whereas some things are always the same, others are always variable. Each sunset is different, each spring, each day. How many times have you said: "I've never seen a sky like this before!" or "There's never been anything like this before!" or "I can't ever remember a spring such as this!"?

There are those who look without seeing, hear without listening, taste without savoring, feel without responding. Raindrops on the window are only a warning to take umbrella and rubbers. They only know that the song of birds awakens them too early summer mornings. A field of fall blooms merely inspires an allergic sneeze. They are casual about fragrant odors and offended by the unpleasant. Children of Nature they may be, but unappreciative, intolerant children, showing no gratitude, offering no praise.

Observe them closely. Pity them. They are not the world's happiest creatures. They live in a drab colorless world full of troublesome irritations.

On the other hand, there are those who never grew too old to enjoy the gifts of Nature. That they may never learn the name of the star which has caught their rapt attention is not important. It matters only that they saw its beauty. They may not be able to identify the bird whose song has thrilled them to a sudden stop or the name of the wild flower whose perfection they have stopped to admire. What is important is that they listened—they stopped to look. It is only when we no longer take time to appreciate the beauty around us that life loses meaning.

Parents who take the time to keep alive the most wonderful quality of childhood—that electric interest in everything—do their children the greatest service. Parents who have themselves maintained that quality that makes the commonplace ever new and full of wonder have found for themselves the secret of good living. They are passing on the secret to their offspring.

NATURE LESSONS IN THE HOME

No matter where a family lives, objects through which Nature teaches us some of her most inspiring secrets can be brought into the home. Some suggestions are given here.

Sundial Experiment

In ancient times, man's only timekeeper was the sundial. The simplest type which can be made needs only a stick. A part of a broom handle or mop stick will suffice. Drive it into the ground at an angle that is equal to the latitude in which you are living. Check on any map to see between which parallels your city is located. Thus if you live in the forty-second parallel the stick must be at a forty-two-degree angle. The upper end of the stick must point to the North Star which is true north. You can locate the North Star by first locating the Big Dipper. The two stars in the bowl of the Big Dipper (in the constel-

lation Ursa Major) point directly to the North Star which is the end of the handle of the Little Dipper (Ursa Minor). When you have placed the stick in the ground, you have placed the gnomon of the sundial. Its shadows will give you accurate time.

If you want to make a more elaborate sundial, construct one similar to that shown in the sketch above. Wood, metal, plastics or almost any material can be used. Mount it in your yard where it will be in the sun for the entire day. If it is in the shade part of the day, it will, of course, not be effective then.

Fun with Plants

One need not have a large garden area to experiment with beauty that grows. Any window sill which receives sunlight some part of the day is all one needs. As a matter of fact, not even direct sunlight is needed in many cases.

An empty tin can, flower pot or decorative ceramic piece filled with soil is the garden plot. Seeds from peas, oranges, lemons, grapefruit, pears or apples will sprout readily. Avacado may be a little more difficult but the end result is beautiful. Jersey sweet potatoes or yams when placed in a jar with water will sprout quickly and produce beautiful hanging plants.

The tops of carrots or beets placed in a shallow dish with a little water will send up shoots in a hurry and make an interesting little dish garden.

Potted plants which can be purchased in florist shops or variety stores come in many varieties. Sansevieria grows tall and straight while ivy varieties and philodendron will climb and twine or fall gracefully in beautiful patterns. Begonias need sun to keep their leaves colorful. Cactus plants of dozens of varieties will go a long time between waterings and will produce colorful blooms. African violets which come in many colors and varieties are a popular and beautiful house plant. Plants, like people, have their own idiosyncrasies which require humoring, but they will reward their owners with beauty if given proper care.

If you pick your dandelions carefully, you can find an example of each stage from the earliest bud to the unfurled blossom, to the mature seed.

At the bottom of each blossom is a white button-like structure. This is the torus. Each seed as it departs from the torus leaves a little pockmark or dimple. If you count the dimples you can see how many seeds it held before they matured and sailed away.

Examine a seed. It has its own parachute. Blow it and watch it sail and then light. Which part hits the ground? Which end has teeth and in what direction do they point? Are these teeth the anchor which holds the seed to the ground?

Look at another blossom. The green petal-like structures are bracts. When it rains the dandelion just folds up these bracts and covers its flowers and seeds. When the seeds are ripe they spread out into a little white ball and wait for a breeze to catch them and carry them off on their journey to start new dandelions.

Dig up a dandelion and examine the root. It is a spongy structure that gives off a white milk (lactic acid). Rub this on your fingers until it turns black. Does it stretch like rubber?

Take a stem. It gives off a milky juice too. Taste it. Bitter, isn't it? Children sometimes split the stem in several sections at the tip and push them down with their lips. They curl under and form a curious little flower-like structure. The bitter taste of the milk from the stem is not easily forgotten. The yellow blossoms make wonderful filling for mud pies, too!

The leaves have many teeth. The French gave the plant its name. They thought the teeth of the leaves looked like lion's teeth so from *"dent de lion,"* the teeth of the lion, they called it the dandelion.

We dig dandelions from our lawns, others cultivate them for their leaves, blanch them and eat them in salads! Taxicum extract is prepared by pharmacists from this plant and its bitter juice has been used as a remedy for warts! Look for two kinds of dandelion. One is the red-seeded type. It is easy to see we don't need to stray too far to see one of the most interesting plants. Probably because it is so common, we overlook it as a possible treasure chest of information.

Winter Bouquets

Late fall is a good time to gather cuttings for your winter bouquets. Sometimes people spray the leaves and blossoms with colored paints or dip the tips in white paint. But this gilding of the blossom is really unnecessary. Nature has done a good job of making things beautiful. Take a close look and see. Cattails, dried milkweed stalks, Queen

Anne's lace and other grasses and weeds carefully dried will bring you pleasure for many months.

Seedy Weeds for the Birds

Watch which plants the birds are interested in. Take some of these plant cuttings home and put the seeds on your bird feeders for a special treat.

Bird Feeders (Suet Type)

Birds will winter in spots where food is offered over a period of several winters. Bird lovers have spent many a happy and informa-

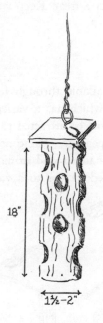

tive hour watching their feeders. And you don't know you are a bird lover until you've watched the birds in action. Put up a feeder and see how long it takes them to convert you.

Such feeders are simple to make. Take a piece of two-by-four of yellow pine about eighteen inches long or a length of a tree branch three or more inches in diameter and about eighteen inches long. With a three-quarter-inch wood bit, drill holes into the wood, angling the bit downward toward the bottom end. Drill the holes one to one and a half inches deep. Nail a flat piece of wood cut square or round on the top to serve as a roof. Put a large screw eye in the top and attach a piece of wire. A piece of coat hanger wire will serve nicely. The more rustic-looking the feeder is, the better. Fill the holes with pieces of suet or peanut butter mixed with corn meal. Hang from the branch of a tree or under the eaves being careful to select a spot where cats cannot reach it and where you can observe it conveniently from your home. It may take the birds a while to find it but when they do they are not the only ones to get a treat. Keep your binoculars and a bird identification book handy.

Seed-Type Feeder

Seed-type feeders are available through feed stores or department stores. Buy wild bird seed which has a variety of types of seeds in it so that all types of birds will be attracted to it. Be sure the mix contains sunflower seeds and peanuts. These are especially attractive to the bluejays, cardinals, nuthatches and titmice.

Hang or mount your feeder close to a vantage point for you but

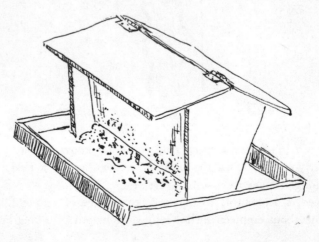

safe from cats. Squirrels can be a nuisance too. Try to feed them at another place so that they will let the bird feeder alone.

Bird Dust Bath

Birds who winter in the North where snow is on the ground a good part of the time and places to take a dust bath are scarce need help from bird lovers. Dust baths help a bird to keep free of lice. A simple wood tray kept filled with powdered earth or fine sand will be a welcome spot to the birds. Like the feeders, place it out of reach of cats.

Bird Baths

Bird baths can be purchased ready-made or can be constructed easily from a length of sewer tile and a metal lid from a barrel or storage drum. Place the bath where cats cannot get at it. Keep it filled with clean fresh water.

Winter Wonder Garden

In the late fall, take the family on a hunting expedition that will bring beauty to your winter window sill garden. Take a trowel or shovel, several four- or five-inch flower pots and a wild flower book to help you with identification. Try to find yarrow for one pot. Yarrow is a common herb whose pink or white blossoms grow in small clusters. The finely divided leaves have a strong smell and taste.

Queen Anne's lace (wild carrot) is another beauty for your wonder winter garden. Its blossoms are white and lacy. Field daisies, pennyroyal (a fuzzy, hairy, tasty member of the mint family), oxalis (garden sorrel), a shamrock-like plant which has white or red blossoms, or St.-John's-wort bring color and interest to your window sill.

Dandelion Adventure

Dandelion plants are as beautiful as any plant you might buy and are a study in themselves. The blossom of gold is in reality a bouquet of blossoms. Each little strap which you have probably thought to be a petal is a blossom in itself. Examine a blossom closely. Pull one of the straps free and examine it carefully under a hand lens. See how many teeth it has at one end. This will tell you the number of petals its ancestor had. Two little "horns" are visible at the top of the flower. These are the stigmas which catch the pollen that is brought by the insects from other plants. Ten stamens make up a collar just below the stigmas. If you touch the stamens with your finger, you will find the pollen which is carried by the insects.

NATURE TRIPS RIGHT AROUND HOME

City Street Geology Trip

Armed with a bit of knowledge, a magnifying glass and an alert observing mind, we have all we need for a geology field trip on any city street.

Begin right where you are, on the sidewalk. Is it man-made recently of concrete or is it one of sandstone formed millions of years ago on the floor of the sea? If it is the latter, examine it for possible ripple marks made by those ancient waters.

Take a look at the gravel driveway. Is it composed of slag which comes from the waste materials drained off molten steel? Then it's man-made material. Or is it composed of little round pebbles of quartz and other rock fragments? These may have come from some river bed or beach. The roundness of the pebbles suggests that water has been at work wearing down the corners and rounding off the edges.

What are your city's curbstones composed of? Are they sandstone, concrete or granite? Granite is older than sandstone. It comes from a magna (molten rock deep in the earth) which has cooled to form granite, an igneous rock. Thus granite has been formed by fire. Sandstone, on the other hand, is a form of sedimentary rock formed by layers and layers of material deposited by wind and water. In the case of sandstone the material was sand.

Thus, without having to stray from our own block, we can learn about man-made materials such as concrete and slag and natural materials, sedimentary or igneous in origin.

As we move farther along we examine building materials. Here's a building with a base of polished granite. Pink granite has crystals of quartz and feldspar so coarse they may be as large as a dime or quarter. Gray granite is finer. Examine it with your magnifying glass. See how the shining surfaces are composed of feldspar and mica. Feldspar is a crystalline mineral, usually aluminum silicate. It is moderately hard and quite glassy and is generally found in igneous rock. Mica is also a silicate but is composed of a group of mineral silicates. It forms crystals that are thin, flexible, translucent and sometimes transparent. These crystals separate easily into layers. Sheets of mica are used in oven doors. Since mica is flame-resistant as well as translucent it is used in electrical appliances, toasters particularly. It is also used as an electrical insulating material. When transparent, mica is called isinglass.

If in our travels we see limestone building blocks, our magnifying glass may reveal fossils of minute sea creatures. Limestone in its pure form (carbonate of lime) is white. Iron and other impurities will give it red, green, brown and blue tints. Chalk is limestone. It can be white, yellow or gray. Chalk is soft, easily pulverized and is composed almost entirely of small seashells. If limestone is composed of almost equal parts of magnesium and carbonate of lime, it becomes dolomite. It is used in the production of steel and as a building material.

When limestone is subjected to heat, pressure or chemical action (known as the process of metamorphism) it becomes marble. Marble is the hard rock used chiefly for ornamental purposes in building. It takes a high polish. Its color may vary from black to white. In Devon and Derbyshire marbles, the markings are due to fossil contents. Italian marbles are used for statuary purposes. Onyx marble comes from Algeria; green serpentinous (looking like a snakeskin) marble comes from Italy, Greece and Ireland. (So that's what happened to the snakes in Ireland!) Vermont is the best source of marble in the United States.

See the bags of sand from some sand dune or beach piled over there? They will be mixed with cement to pour in the foundation of that building there. Cement is composed of powdered clay and lime. When limestone is subjected to heat, naturally or by man, lime results. Lime is used in making plaster of Paris and cement and for treating soil.

Bricks are a story in themselves. They are made from clay. And what is clay? It is a fine-grained earth, composed chiefly of aluminum silicates. Haven't we mentioned that substance before? Feldspar found in granite is an aluminum silicate. When feldspar or mica weather to dust after being embedded in ancient seas, they become clay. Clay when mixed with water and fired into a brick or a tile becomes a man-made igneous rocklike formation. And thus the cycle is complete again but this time with man taking a hand in the process.

We look in a store window and see china and pottery pieces—more clay mixed, shaped and fired. The glass through which we look is made from sand and other silicates. The addition of various chemical compounds produces glass of different colors and qualities. Some glass can be used to bake and cook foods in. Glass can be blown into various shapes, rolled into sheets or shaped into various forms. It is used for everyday objects and is made into beautiful art objects. It was first known in Egypt forty centuries ago.

In a drugstore window we see talcum powder made of talc, one of the softest rocks. There is a box of wax crayons so dear to a child's heart. Talc is used to make them too.

Around the world we go in a jewelry store window. Here are diamonds from South Africa, fire opals from Mexico, rubies from Burma, turquoise from our own Southwest or even Persia. Radium, that radioactive metallic chemical element which comes from pitchblende and other uranium materials, glows in the dark on the hands and numerals of alarm clocks and watches. In the same window are precious metals, gold, platinum and silver from all over the world.

In the hardware window are products made from iron, copper, aluminum, tin and chromium. India and Turkey send us chromium. Tungsten in our electric bulbs comes from China, Argentina or Bolivia. The mercury in the thermometer may have come from Italy and the magnesium in another product from our own Western mountains.

Let's go back a million years or so when there were forests of giant ferns and club mosses. They're right here in this lump of coal, in this bit of polished diamond in our ring, in the oil we put into our cars or the gas with which we cook our dinner.

Thus in the time it takes to walk around the block, we've traveled around the world. We've had a geology field trip. We've studied history (both political and natural), commercial geography and industry. In a few minutes, we've covered thousands of miles and bridged a million years. And that's not all. Junior and Susie have been exposed to many fascinating facts—among them being that Dad and Mom are pretty smart people—fun to know and fun to be with. And Dad and Mom? They've learned something too. They've learned that doing things together as a family can be quite a wonderful experience, exciting, exhilarating and heart-warming. Without going far, without spending a dime (unless they all stop for a soda at the corner drugstore) an experience that will be treasured for years to come can be crowded into one fun-packed, fact-filled hour.

SEEDS—MIRACLES IN MINIATURE

Two thousand years ago Jesus likened the kingdom of God unto a seed. He said: "The Kingdom of God is like to a grain of mustard seed, which a man took and sowed in his field: which indeed is the least of all seeds: but when it is grown, it is the greatest among herbs, and becometh a tree, so the birds of the air come and lodge in the branches thereof."

A small seed which grows to such magnitude is no less remarkable to us now despite our increased scientific knowledge. Yet the fact that such a tiny object can grow so big is only one of its remarkable features.

Each seed no matter how small contains a microscopic plant complete with root, stalk and leaf. Each seed carries its own food supply. Any one of these features—the living part or germ, the built-in food supply, the method by which it travels, the manner in which seeds grow—is a study in itself.

The living part, the germ, can stay alive for a long time waiting for favorable conditions to grow. Usually a seed waits from summer until spring. Some grass and weed seeds may germinate after ten or fifteen years.

A whole world of wonder is contained in a seed. There are countless varieties of all sizes and shapes. They travel in many ways, by air, water, inside birds or just drop to the ground. Each seed is an efficient machine, a masterpiece of design and contains the miracle of life.

Families on nature walks in parks or fields, in their homes or own back yards can spend hour upon hour studying, observing, experimenting with seeds. There is always something new to learn, wonderful to see, exciting to behold. This is a study that need have no end. Its possibilities are wonderfully endless.

Seeds are an important source of food for all living things. At dinner some night, play a game trying to name all the different seeds which have been used in the preparation of that meal. The list will be longer than you will at first guess. Just for fun, some night at dinner have each member of the family venture a guess as to the number of different seeds eaten during that day. Record each guess for the record and then collectively make up a list. See which member of the family comes closest to the total. Here is a list to help you in compiling yours:

> Lima, navy, string or kidney beans
> Black-eyed, green or yellow peas
> Rice, barley, buckwheat, wheat, corn, soybean, rye, oats, wild rice
> Walnuts, pecans, peanuts, coconuts, cashews, almonds, chestnuts, brazil nuts
> Anise, caraway, cardamon, celery, cumin, dill, fennel, mustard, nutmeg, pepper (red, black or white), poppy seed, sesame, vanilla, chocolate
> Pomegranates, strawberries, blackberries, raspberries (try eating these without eating the seeds), green grapes
> Coffee, coffee substitutes made from grains

If we were to list foods made from seeds or seed products our list is infinitely longer. For example:

> Breads and flour products: pancakes, breads and rolls,

macaroni, noodles, spaghetti, cakes, cookies, pies, cereals, dumplings

Fats and oils

Oleomargarine (cottonseed or soybean)

Cooking and salad oils, cottonseed and olive oil

Vegetables: It would be almost impossible to eat cucumber, tomatoes, okra without eating the seeds. In corn on the cob we eat only the seeds.

Fruits: When we eat grapes, berries, pomegranates, we eat the seeds, too.

Candy and confections: Imagine candy without chocolate, vanilla or almond flavoring. Popcorn is all seed.

Take seeds and seed products from our diets and we wouldn't have too much left. True, we'd have meats, dairy products and seafoods, but the animals we eat depend upon seeds and grasses grown from seeds for their diets. Take away the seeds which give flavor and variety to our foods and our meals would be monotonous in taste and appearance. Rolls topped with nuts, poppy seed or sesame seed look and taste better. Imagine apple pie without spices, cakes and cookies without flavoring and nuts, relishes without spices and condiments. Eating wouldn't be nearly so much fun. Yes indeed, seeds contribute much to our lives.

SEEDS AND HOW THEY ARE MADE

The seed is the cause of much plant activity. All spring, summer and fall plants are hard at work carrying on the activities which produce seeds. Thousands of miles of hairlike roots push their way through all types of soil, hard and obstinate or soft and yielding, to gather, filter and lift gallons of solution. Leaves grow and produce food. Plants flower in wood and field, their petals and stamens carrying out their duties while countless thousands of pollen grains are distributed.

Once the seed is produced and sent on its way to bring forth other plants, the plant takes a rest. Leaves fall off, the flowers fade and stems shrivel. Where there were once intense activity, bright colors and heavy foliage, there is now dinginess and drabness and what appears to be lifelessness. Actually life is now scaled down to such minute proportions it is hardly perceptible. It is as if the plants having done their assigned tasks had now taken a vacation. The millions of seeds they have produced have dropped to the ground or sailed off on the winds to new homes to begin to grow as soon as the conditions are favorable. When the vacation is over, many of the plants will begin their work again to repeat the process of seed making.

In the season when the plant is in flower the ovary of the flower becomes the compartment in which the seeds are housed. This ovary usually clings to the seed. Sometimes as it develops it grows wings, as it does in the seeds of the ash or maple, or it may turn into a crab apple, a blackberry, a nut or a capsule.

SEED PODS AND HOW THEY OPERATE

Each plant has its own machine shop which installs the mechanisms for distributing its seed. When the product is ready, the shop goes into mass production. The plant housing this efficient shop may be dry and brittle and appear to be dead. Actually the seed containers have no living cells. They operate like miniature machines but they need no human hand to operate them. They seem endowed with the capacity to go into action when the time is right; i.e., when the seed is ripe.

The seed case must mature its seed before it can open. Then it may open at the top, side or bottom. It may release its seeds by opening a trap door, lifting up a hinged lid or by rolling back the walls. The size of the seeds and the way they are attached determines the capacity of the seed case, the shape and the method by which it expels the seeds.

If the seeds have not matured because of some accident or have been eaten by larvae before they are ripe, the pod will not open and the ejection machinery never goes into operation.

The Milkweed Zipper Seed Case

The milkweed operates on a zipper-like principle. A line down one side separates by rolling back its lips from top to bottom. The seeds are arranged in a compact spiral and peel off one by one and travel to their destination by parachute. They do not merely drop off to the ground. They remain attached by the tip of the parachute until a breeze comes along and proves it is strong enough to pull the seed loose from its mooring and carry it off on its back.

The Witch Hazel Duck Bill Seed Pod

The seeds of the witch hazel bush are contained in heavy pods with two thick lips. These pods grow on the branches at the same time the bush is bearing yellow flowers. The flowers are the beginnings of the seed pods which will mature the following fall! When the weather combinations are just exactly right, the seed pod will open up like a duck's bill (drawing on left) and the little oval-shaped seeds shoot out like bullets from a gun, flying as far as six feet!

The Touch-Me-Not Mainspring Seed Case

The touch-me-not or jewelweed seed pod has five mainsprings. These are strap-shaped and form the segments of the seed pod. They

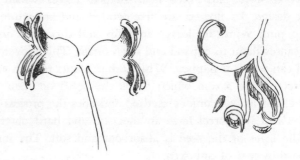

fit perfectly together and are cemented together with some of nature's special glue which makes the pod waterproof but interferes in no way with the spring mechanism. As the pod grows and the straps elongate, they become tense as a stretched rubber band. When touched, the pressure is relaxed and the springs curl up releasing the seeds with a tiny explosion. If you touch a seed pod it explodes so violently the seeds will be gone before you see them. All that may remain in your hand are the curled-up mainsprings (drawing on right).

But nature does not rely on your hand to spring the mechanism. The seed pod is more carefully engineered than to trust to accident to release its seeds. The pod has within it a core to which five seeds are attached at equally spaced intervals around and down the length. The tip of the core is attached at the point where tips of the mainsprings are joined together. The core is at first attached to the stem from which it gathers its nourishment to build the seeds. When the seeds are mature the core is loosened from the stem. The bases of the springs however are still attached to the stem. This attachment grows weaker and weaker and the pull of the springs grows stronger and stronger. When the seeds are fully ripe, the glue at the base of the springs cannot withstand the pull of the springs any longer. The whole pod lets go and takes off like a rocket. While it is still in the air, the violent action of the uncoiling springs knocks out the seeds which fly in all directions.

The Wood Sorrel Do-It-Yourself Seed Case

The wood sorrel has three heart-shaped leaves which make a shamrock design. Its flowers are five-petaled and are white or pink with deep pink veins. Its leaves fold up and droop at night until daylight causes them to expand and open again. This movement is so rapid you can watch it happen. While other plants rely on an outside force to set off the action which sends the seeds on their way, the wood sorrel has its own unique method and does the process all itself.

The seeds of the sorrel have an inelastic and hard outer coating. The middle layer of the seed is absorbent and soft. The inner layer is like the thin coat of any seed.

Three days before the seed is fully ripe, the water in the plant, as if on a mysterious signal, shifts within the plant. The stem swells up to almost double its size. The outside layer of the seed coat loses water and contracts to one-third its size. The inside layer takes on water and swells, resisting the contraction of the outer layer. With the outside pushing against the inside and the inside putting up terrific resistance something has to give. Bang! The seed case turns almost inside out expelling the seed leaving the capsule which held it hanging limp and tired on its stem.

A Family Seed Hike

In the fall when seeds are maturing, the family armed with a wild flower book and a magnifying glass can take off for the fields and woods hunting all types of seed pods and cases. See how many different types you can find. Take samples home to examine at your leisure. Try to find full as well as empty seed cases from trees, grasses, fruit trees, berry bushes, wild flowers and weeds.

Try to figure out by what method each seed was expelled. Try to identify the method by which each seed traveled. Which is the smallest seed you can find? Which is the largest? Try to get some of the seeds to grow in your home.

In the next few pages you will find information about the methods by which seeds travel or are transported from the original plant to another spot where they may take root if the conditions are favorable.

SEEDS AND HOW THEY TRAVEL

Seeds travel by as many methods as people. It is fun to compare their methods to our own. Some are adventuresome and want to get

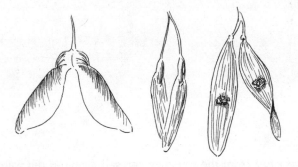

as far away from their parent plants as possible while others are content to set up housekeeping as close to Mama and Papa as possible. Some travel by mechanical means, by wing or propellor, some go by airship, some by water, others by four-legged vehicles. Amazing? Remarkable? Take a field trip and see how amazing and remarkable seeds really are.

The Seed Air Force

The maple, the ash and ailanthus are some of the members of the seed air force. The maple and ash develop wings by which they go whirling through the air using the wind as motors. The ailanthus has a propellor and also uses a wind motor. Gather up a handful of this type of seeds and throw them into the air. Watch how they whirl and glide on the air currents.

The Seed Merchant Marine

Ever notice how the coconut tree leans? Since many grow by a river or shore, they lean over the water so that when their seeds

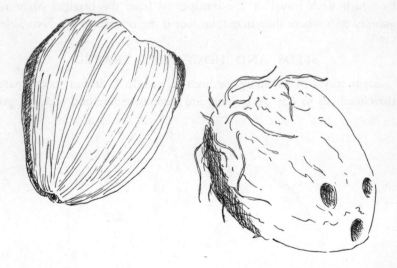

(coconuts) fall from the tree they can sail away on the water to begin their new homes. Here is a shipbuilding establishment that launches its own ships without benefit of champagne and speeches.

A lotus and other water-lily-type plants have seed pods looking like the nozzle of a sprinkling can that take to the water like ducks and swim away to start their new lives in faraway places.

Seed Hitchhikers

Some seeds wait for some person or animal to come along to hitch a ride on. Unlike human hitchhikers, they don't have to wait for the passing vehicle to stop and ask them to come aboard, they just grab at a likely spot and hang on. You've probably given many cockleburs,

the nozzle of a sprinkling can that take to the water like ducks and then had a time getting them out of your clothes. Animals passing by are apt to give free rides unwillingly to these hitchhikers in their fur. Has your dog ever come home from a run in the fields and whiningly asked you to remove cockleburs from his coat or paws?

Seed Paratroopers

The dandelion and milkweed seeds travel by parachute. Amazingly enough, these seeds know when to jump and when not to. In wet weather the dandelion just folds up until weather conditions are better. Then it opens up and lets the wind take its seeds for a ride. The milkweed doesn't just drop off when it is ripe, it waits for the wind to come by and carry it away.

These hairlike processes on the seeds of dandelions, milkweeds, cattails, asters, goldenrods and hawkweeds are called the pappi. In all cases the pappi will stay closed in wet weather. On a dry day when the wind is favorable a city or countryside will look as if it has been hit by a snowstorm, the air will be so full of "seed troopers." If that is the day you chose to paint your house, oh, my!

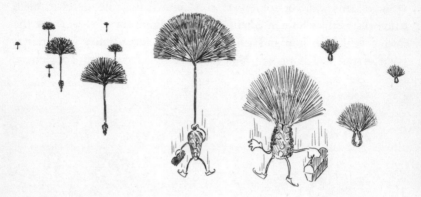

Seed Travelers by Freight Express

The seeds of the various grasses, grains and berries choose to travel by freight methods. Some travel as cargo inside birds. Birds like to eat berries. The seeds pass through the alimentary canal of these flying freight carriers and fall to the ground in bird droppings and are scattered over a wide area.

The grass seeds rely on gravity or nature's down elevator. They just fall to the ground on a quiet day and set up housekeeping close

by if they are the type who chose to stay near home. What's good enough for Papa and Mama is good enough for them. The more adventuresome type may hitch a ride on a passing breeze and move to the suburbs to make their home.

The seeds of many grasses are eaten by animals and like the berry seeds pass through the alimentary canal of the animals and are distributed by means of the animal dung. We might say, they moved to their new homes as cargo on four-legged moving vans.

The Seed Artillery

Some seeds start life off with a bang. The witch hazel, jewelweed, violet and geranium have mechanisms which literally explode and shoot out their seeds like projectiles. Like the man in the circus who allows himself to be shot from a gun these seeds apparently enjoy living dangerously.

The Seed Enticers

Some seeds use enticing methods to get where they want to go. The anemone and hellebores equip their seeds with oil which ants like. The ants carry the seeds off into their homes. What does a seed do when it is in the ground? Grow, of course, what else?

Acorns, nuts of all types and the seeds in pine and cones are very good to eat, at least the squirrels, chipmunks and other rodents think so. These animals gather up hundreds of this type seed and eat some and hide away others for a rainy or wintry day. Sometimes they forget where they have hidden them and so these seeds so neatly planted in the ground by chipmunk and squirrel farmers begin to grow just as if that were the way the animal planned it. Actually the squirrels and chipmunks shouldn't care. What if the seed they planted for food grows instead? It will only grow up into a tree which produces more food, so there is no loss!

SEEDS AND HOW THEY GROW

Like any world traveler, seeds need food to survive. Mother Nature doesn't rely on her seed children finding a drive-in or a swank restaurant to satisfy their needs. Each seed carries his own breakfasts, lunches, dinners and snacks, especially packed by its mother plant. There is just enough to last until the seed settles down in its new home.

Each seed as we have mentioned before has a germ—that living miracle in miniature which contains a microscopic plant complete with root, stem and leaf. This plant is nourished by the built-in food supply which lasts until the new plant has taken root and can make its own food.

Seed Germination Experiment

Place some lima beans on some gauze or cotton in a shallow dish of water. Watch the beans swell and sprout and begin to grow. You can see the tiny plant which was wrapped up in the seed coat with its two packages of food. Place some of the seeds in soil and watch the growth from day to day. Soon the plants will be making their own food. The larger the plant grows, the smaller become the food packets until they finally disappear.

The lima bean is a green plant and like all this variety of plant it has the skill and ability to make its own food. It does this by taking the water and minerals from the soil and carbon dioxide from the air. With the help of the green chlorophyll in the leaves and the energy from the sun it produces sugar. Later this sugar is converted to starch, oils, fats and proteins. While doing all this, the green plant liberates oxygen, releases moisture to the air which travels upward to become a cloud which returns this moisture to the earth in rain. Now, what more could you ask of one little plant? In addition, this plant is making seeds which can become new plants or can be used by animals or humans as food. Truly plants and seeds are wondrous things.

FAMILY NATURE GAMES

Food Geography

At dinner some night, play a game of food geography. Go around the table from one member to another. Each in turn names a food he likes and the country or part of the world from which it comes. The lists will be long and excitingly informative. Give a prize of an extra dessert to the member who can name the most foods and their origins accurately.

Here is a list to use as a reference guide.

Coffee: Brazil, Java, Arabia (mocha)

Teas: India, Ceylon, China, Japan, Formosa

Sugar cane: Cuba, Philippines, Louisiana

Pineapple: Hawaii, Cuba

Olive: Italy, Greece, France, Spain

Citrus fruits: Texas, Florida, California

Apples: Oregon, Ohio, Washington

Peaches: Georgia, Ohio

Spices: West Indies, South America, East Indies, Tropical
    Asia and the Malay Archipelago

"What Are We Eating?" Quiz

Try this on the family some evening at dinner. See if the members can identify which part of the plant they are eating. The correct answer is italicized.

1. Cauliflower, broccoli and artichoke are:
   a. the stem *b. the flowers c.* the root
2. Peas, beans, coffee are:
   a. roots *b.* seed pods *c.* fruit *d. seeds*
3. Spinach, parsley, lettuce, cabbage are:
   a. leaves b. stems *c.* roots
4. Onions are:
   a. underground stems *b. bulbs c.* roots
5. Radishes, carrots, beets, parsnips are:
   a. stems *b.* bulbs *c. roots*
6. Pumpkins, squash, tomatoes, cucumbers are:
   a. stems *b.* roots *c. fruits d.* flowers
7. Celery, leeks are:
   a. leaves *b. stalks c.* fruits
8. White potatoes are:
   a. roots *b. underground stems c.* bulbs

9. Asparagus is:

    a. stalk b. stem *c.* leaves

10. Brussels sprouts are:

    a. stem *b. sprouts growing on the stem c.* flowers

11. Kale is:

    a. flowers *b.* leaves *c. stems and leaves*

Common Foods and Their Origins

Listed below are common foods and the families from which they come. The lists are scrambled. See if you can unscramble them. To play this as a dinner table game some night as a family stunt, let one member read off the names of the foods one at a time going around the table from one member to another as is done in a spelling bee. If the first person cannot give the family name, go on to the next. See who gets the most right.

FOOD	FAMILY NAME
1. Apple	a. Almond
2. Peach	b. Palm
3. Date	c. Evergreen and cashew
4. Mango	d. Rose
5. Tangelo	e. Hybrid of orange and grapefruit
6. Grapefruit	f. Nightshade
7. Tangerine	g. Cactus
8. Prickly pear	h. Apple
9. Pear	i. Orchid
10. Vanilla	j. Wild carrot
11. Tomato	k. Wild sea cabbage
12. Potato	l. Dill, caraway
13. Carrot	m. Mustard
14. Cabbage	n. Pumpkin
15. Celery	o. Lily
16. Radish	p. Orange
17. Squash	q. Orange and lemon
18. Onion	r. Evergreen
19. Olive	

Answers: 1-d, 2-a, 3-b, 4-c, 5-e, 6-q, 7-p, 8-g, 9-h, 10-i, 11-f, 12-f, 13-j, 14-k, 15-l, 16-m, 17-n, 18-o, 19-r.

"Vegetable, Animal or Mineral" Quiz Game

Everything in the world is either vegetable, animal or mineral. It is fun to try to match the correct classification with a common food or something which we use in everyday living. Some are easily identified, but some make us stop a minute and think. Families could play at the quiz below to see how good they are at matching.

CLASSIFICATION

a. Vegetable   b. Animal   c. Mineral   d. Combination of vegetable and animal   e. Combination of vegetable and mineral f. Combination of vegetable and animal and mineral   g. Combination of animal and mineral

FOOD OR THING

1. Milk
2. Tea
3. Water
4. Leather shoes
5. Tennis shoes
6. Salt
7. Rope
8. Plastics
9. Nylons
10. Cotton sheet
11. Pepper
12. Sugar
13. Rubber band
14. Paper clip
15. Silk
16. Yeast
17. Cheese
18. Automobile

19. Glass
20. Cake
21. Bread
22. Mushroom soup
23. Pencil
24. Honey
25. Maple syrup
26. Zipper cotton jacket
27. Brick
28. Crayons
29. Chalk
30. Wicker basket
31. Bamboo drapes
32. Butter
33. Salad oil
34. Gas-filled balloon
35. All-day sucker on a wooden stick

Answers: 1-b, 2-a, 3-c, 4-f, 5-a, 6-c, 7-a, 8-a, 9-c, 10-a, 11-a, 12-a, 13-a, 14-c, 15-b, 16-a, 17-d, 18-f, 19-c, 20-f, 21-f, 22-d, 23-e, 24-d, 25-a, 26-e, 27-c, 28-c, 29-c, 30-a, 31-a, 32-b, 33-a, 34-e, 35-a.

VARIATION

Make a set of flash cards each of which bears the name of a classification or a combination of classifications. Have one member of the
family flash the cards, shuffling them occasionally so no one will
know which card is coming up next. The first member to name a
correct item which fits the classification gets a point. The first
member to get ten points is card flasher for the next round.

FAMILY PROJECTS FOR HOME NATURE STUDY

Fun with Plants

Terrarium

A terrarium is simply a miniature garden under glass. A layer of
moist soil covered with moss to prevent evaporation will support
plant life as well as insects, frogs, snakes, lizards or other harmless
wild things.

The container for this garden may be a flower pot filled with

soil and covered with moss with a lantern globe or a lamp chimney
for the glass part. This is covered either with cheesecloth to prevent
the insects from getting out, or a lid of glass.

It is wise as well as kindly not to keep any living specimen too
long as snakes, frogs and lizards do better in their natural environ-

ment. Even if you attempt to simulate their home environment as closely as possible, it is at best an imitation home-away-from-home for these creatures.

Much can be learned from the study of life in a single terrarium. The more elaborate terrarium however can be made into an attractive addition to the home as well as an efficient receptacle for study.

Use a rectangular-shaped fish aquarium which can be purchased or made as a container for the terrarium. The possibilities for variations are numerous. Some suggestions follow:

The Woodland Garden

Take a clean container. For a foundation, use a layer of clean gravel or broken flower pots and cover this with two or three inches

of sand for good drainage. Bits of charcoal mixed with the sand will help to keep the soil sweet. Now add a two-inch layer of slightly sandy garden soil that has been sifted and dampened. It is damp enough if it will hold together when squeezed in your hands. Build up the soil in spots to make the topography interesting with little hills and valleys. Rocks which are weathered or lichen-covered can be used to simulate cliffs. A miniature pond can be made of a shallow glass dish which you can sink into the soil to make it more realistic. Place a circlet of pebbles around the plate to keep the moss from absorbing all the water. An odd-shaped piece of weather-beaten wood will add to the beauty of your garden.

You are ready now to plant your tree seedlings and small plants which you have gathered. Some suggested plants are Christmas fern, partridge berry, club mosses, plantain and evergreen seedlings. Seedlings of hemlock, acorn maple, tulip and sassafras are fun to watch grow.

Use tiny or small plants whose leaves do not reach to the glass. Set the plantlings out to simulate a woodland scene. Then cover the soil with a layer of moss. Select different kinds of moss, but try to get mosses that grow on the ground rather than those you find on rotting wood or bark. This latter type does not do too well in a terrarium.

Having planted your terrarium, wet it down with a fine spray of water. A window sprayer will do nicely. Do not wet to the saturation point. Set a glass cover on loosely so that air can circulate. Keep in a cool place and not in direct sunlight. Keep the glass clean. Watch for leaves that are turning yellow and plants that are dying. Remove these as soon as possible. If droplets of water appear in abundance remove the cover for a couple of hours until most of the condensation evaporates. If the plants look dry and no condensation appears, spray the garden. Once a month should be enough to spray but each garden requires different care. Watch the glass walls for evidence of too much or too little condensation and judge the need for water accordingly.

The City Garden Terrarium

Make the foundation for a city garden the same as that of the woodland garden substituting potting soil for the sandy garden soil. Buy or obtain from your friends slips and tiny plants of begonia, croton, baby tears, oxalis, peperomia, grape ivy and myrtle for the plants. You are not limited to these, of course. Plant your favorite type plant and see what happens. As in the woodland garden use small plants whose leaves will not reach the top of the glass. Give them a chance to grow that high and watch them while they do. Once a plant gets too large it is wise to replace it with small ones.

The Desert Garden

Put a layer of pebbles and dry sand about three inches deep in the bottom of your terrarium and cover with three inches or more of sandy potting mixture. Arrange so that the surface has a dry gully or arroyo running through it. Plant with potted succulents, cacti, sedums and aloes. It seems to work better if the plants are buried pot and all though you may want to try planting without the pots taking care not to disturb the roots or the soil of the plant before setting it into the soil of your desert garden.

Keep in a sunny warm spot. Spray the soil around the plants taking care not to spray the plants themselves or the rest of the sand. About once a week is ample watering.

Nature Flash Card Games

There is an old saying that we "learn to swim in winter and ice skate in summer." We can learn many interesting facts about identifying trees, birds, wild flowers and constellations at home by playing flash card games. (You can make your own cards or purchase them at bookstores or your natural history museum.) Then when the time is right to go out into the woods or fields we can more easily identify the things we see. Being able to call a wild flower by name or identify a bird in flight is more than fun. It makes you feel so smart!

Bird Flash Game

Take three- by five-inch filing cards. Paste a picture on each card of one of the birds you are apt to see in the region where you live. On the back of the card list the following: name of bird, color or colors of the male, size, color of female, simple description of the kind of song or call the bird has, where and what time of year you are most apt to see such a bird.

Have one person flash the cards one by one before the family. The person identifying the bird correctly first, wins the card. The person having the most cards at the end of the games flashes them for the next game. In case two players call out the correct name at the same time, the one who can name most of the identifications wins that card.

You will find this game most helpful in training you to make quick and accurate identifications on a bird walk.

Wild Flower Flash Game

Play as in bird flash game. Prepare a set of cards with pictures of the wild flowers common to the woods and fields in the area in which you live. It will be that much more fun when you go into the woods in search of wild flowers to see alive the flowers you have learned to identify by picture. Be sure to include poison ivy and poison oak. These you want to be sure to know.

Constellation Flash Game

Prepare a set of cards as described in the games above. Draw or cut out pictures of the most easily found constellations of both the winter and summer skies. Once you've learned them by card it will be easy to find them in the sky. Include approximate location as well as names of important stars in the constellation on the back of the card for quick reference.

Tree Flash Game

Prepare a set of flash cards with pictures of leaves, pine needles or some other identifying marks of the trees found most commonly in the area in which you live. List the name and other facts of identification on the backs of the cards. If you play this at home often enough you'll find it easier to call a tree by name when you meet it the next time.

Butterfly and Moth Flash Game

In your walks through the woods and fields and around your home you will see many types of butterflies and moths. Make a set of cards picturing the most common types. The information on the backs of the cards should include what type of caterpillars the moths and butterflies emerge from as well as the kind of food they eat. The latter bit of information will help in finding them. (See following section on moths and butterflies in this chapter for some pertinent facts about these insects.)

Fun with Aquatic Plants and Animals

The Home Aquarium

Use any kind of container that is transparent glass, a gallon jar, a fish globe or a rectangular-shaped glass and metal aquarium. The cost of the aquarium in no way determines how much fun the family will get watching the marine life in it. Start out simply. Don't go to great expense. Enthusiasms and interests change. Many people "shoot the works" when they are starting out on a new hobby and then when their interest wanes find themselves with a lot of expensive equipment they no longer want.

Equipping the Aquarium

Place an inch or so of sand, which you have thoroughly cleaned by putting it in a piece of cloth and washing out all the dirt, in the bottom of the container. Small pebbles can be used instead of sand. Put in a few strands of a water weed which grows under water securing the roots in the bottom of the jar. Use water from river, pond or a lake if possible, otherwise city water will be suitable. One stone should come near the top of the surface of the water as some creatures need shallow water in order to live.

Toad or frog eggs are fun to watch. Put a slimy stone, leaf or twig in the container for feeding. Two gallons of water will take care of twenty tadpoles, a small frog, a few water bugs, a small fish and some snails. Don't overcrowd an aquarium. For the fish and frog, a few bread crumbs, a couple of live insects or a small piece of raw meat is sufficient for a day's food supply. Do not leave old food in the aquarium after the creatures have finished feeding. Dip it out with a spoon or a net. Never use your hands. Do not overfeed. Keep the aquarium out of direct sunlight.

A balance of plant and animal life in an aquarium keeps the water clean. If it should get greenish or cloudy change the water.

Moths and Butterflies

Moths and butterflies make interesting study projects the year round for the family which likes to experiment with and observe at close hand some of the fascinating habits of these insects.

Caterpillars of both moths and butterflies can be brought into the house and kept alive in cages where they can be observed during the various stages of their development.

Caterpillar Cages

Almost any glass container which makes observation easy will serve as a cage. Cover the top with screening to keep your specimen in the jar. The top should be easy to remove so that fresh food can be put into the jar when necessary.

When you find the caterpillar that you wish to observe notice what kind of food it is eating when you find it. Provide your captive with fresh leaves from this plant. After a time the caterpillar pupates or hibernates and then it is no longer necessary to feed it. All you have to do is wait until it emerges as a butterfly or moth. In the house, this often happens earlier in the year than it would outside and often before the food it normally eats is available.

If it is a cocoon you are putting in the jar, it does not need food. It just needs to be watched occasionally so that you can see it when the moth or butterfly is ready to emerge.

Gathering Your Specimens

The study of moths and butterflies necessitates the study of caterpillars which are part of the life cycle of these insects. Moths and butterflies have three stages of growth: the egg, the caterpillar or larva, the pupa (chrysalid in the butterfly, cocoon in the moth) stage.

Since the eggs are harder to find and identify, we begin with the study of the caterpillars with summer and early fall being the best time to study this stage of development.

Most caterpillars develop into butterflies or moths, but some are the larva stage of the sawflies which are wasplike insects. Since the mission of the caterpillar is to store food for the pupal or resting stage, they spend most of their time eating. They feed and grow rapidly and may molt from four to ten times, shedding their outer skins when they do.

Caterpillars have a head equipped with a pair of well-developed jaws capable of nipping leaves or gnawing trees and a pair of short bristly antennae. There are usually six eyes on each side of the head just above the base of the jaw. These are beadlike structures so small you will need a hand lens to see them. The eyelike spots you see on

the upper front part of the body are decorations and not really eyes. See if you can spot the real eyes with your lens. Behind the head are three thoracic segments of the body. Each has a pair of true legs. The next nine or ten sections are the abdominal segments. In the caterpillars of moths and butterflies there are never more than five pairs of prolegs attached to these segments each of which has a hook aptly called a crotchet. Measuring worms have only two or three pairs of prolegs while the larvae of sawflies have more than five pairs and these are not equipped with crotchets.

Most caterpillars do not sting or bite people. Some may give off an offensive odor, some are quite beautiful but all are interesting to study. Some appear quite ferocious. If they were ten times or a hundred times bigger we should all be tempted to run at the sight of them. Many are spiny or hairy. This tends to protect them from their animal and bird enemies. The only caterpillars that have hairs that sting and so should be handled carefully are the larvae of the Io moth and the saddleback caterpillar.

Some caterpillars have protective coloring and are hard to see in their natural environment. Measuring worms stand up on their hind prolegs when disturbed and resemble twigs. Larvae of many moths will stand on their rear prolegs and assume a pose when disturbed.

The spicebush swallowtail larva has a forked structure much like a snake's tongue which it thrusts out from a scent gland it has in the upper part of the first segment of its body. When disturbed, out comes the tongue and an unpleasant odor is given off. These skunks of the caterpillar world are harmless to people and develop into beautiful butterflies.

Caterpillars are destructive creatures. Most of them eat plant life. Some eat the edges of leaves, others eat holes in leaves, the carpenter moth bores into wood, the goldenrod gall moth lives in a spindle-shaped gall on the stem of the goldenrod. Look for these galls. Cut one open. See if the larva is still there or has emerged and literally flown his coop.

A caterpillar has a silk gland which is a modified salivary gland that opens on the lower lip. The silkworm moth larva is the only one that makes silk that is commercially useful. Most caterpillars use their silk to spin a cocoon. Some hairy caterpillars like the woolly bears make their cocoons largely from the hairs on their body using very little silk for their cocoons.

Caterpillar shelters or cocoons vary. Some roll up a leaf and tie it in place with silk. Then they lie inside this shelter and feed there, a kind of breakfast-in-bed type. Some butterfly larvae use a leaf shelter just to winter in. Tent caterpillars tie some leaves together with silk and feed within the tent until they are ready to pupate. Other tent caterpillar families may eat outside the tent and use it only as a retreat.

Some caterpillars make a case from pieces of leaves and twigs which they carry around on themselves. Later they pupate in this case. Look in your evergreen shrubbery for such a case. The bagworm is a case-making caterpillar who lives in this type shrub.

Look for moth pupae in the ground, under a stone or a log. Moth pupae are usually dark brown. Butterfly pupae (usually called chrysalids) are variously colored and may be attached by the tail and held in place by a silken girdle or life line to a twig or leaf.

The ground beetle and birds and many other animals eat caterpillars. Some flies and wasps parasitize them. Try and find a tomato worm (larva of the Sphinx moth) which has been attacked by para-

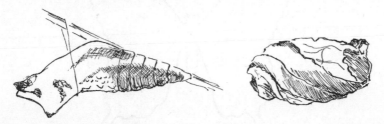

sites. Sometimes the entire body will be covered with tiny cocoons which the parasites have spun.

The parasites lay their eggs on or in the body of the caterpillar. The larvae from these parasites then proceed to make a meal of the insides of the caterpillar. Sometimes the parasites kill off the caterpillar before it can pupate. If it pupates before it is killed, the parasites live in the pupa and emerge from the pupa instead of the butterfly or moth.

Feeding the Captive Caterpillar

If the caterpillar you have found is feeding, note what kind of plant it is eating and continue to feed it a fresh leaf daily until it goes into the pupal stage when it no longer needs food.

The adult moths or butterflies will emerge a month or two earlier inside than they would normally. The adult stage moth or butterfly is more easily identified if one has a good butterfly or moth book.

When the moth or butterfly finally emerges, if you know the difference between a moth and a butterfly, it will help you in identifying it.

The table below will help you in determining whether you have a moth or butterfly.

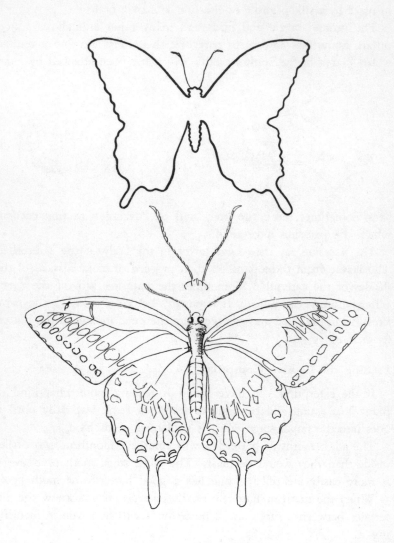

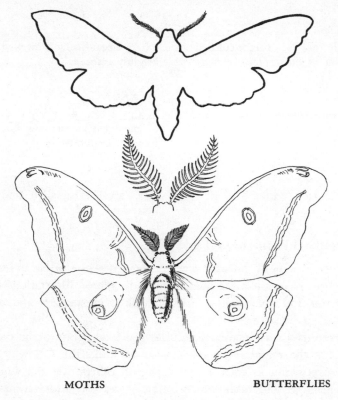

MOTHS	BUTTERFLIES

Antennae

Threadlike	Club-shaped tips always
Feathery	
Spindle-shaped	
Never clublike	

Flight

Usually twilight or evenings	Usually daytime

Wings

Scaly winged (except clear-wing types)	Scaly winged (except clear-wing types)
Usually have fore and hind wings attached by bristle and catch	Fore and hind wing not attached

Colors

Usually not so bright-colored or brilliant as butterflies	Often beautifully marked and brightly colored

Wing Position at Rest

Rest with wings folded	Wings at rest in upright position or expanded horizontally but never folded like moths

Life Cycle

Egg, larval (cocoon) and adult moth	Egg, larval (chrysalid) and adult butterfly

Caterpillar Identification Table

There is actually no easy way to identify a caterpillar unless you happen to have an insect guidebook with colored illustrations handy when you find a caterpillar. Such a book is inexpensive and readily obtained at bookstores.

Caterpillars vary in their life cycles and food habits. Some pass the winter in the pupal stage and emerge as adults the following year. Some overwinter as caterpillars while still others pass the winter in the egg stage. The table which follows gives you information about food plants on which you can find certain types and how the caterpillars pass the winter.

BUTTERFLIES

Caterpillar	Type of Vegetation	Winters
Monarch	Milkweed	Adults migrate south
Viceroy	Poplar trees	Pupa (leaf shelter)
Purples (red-spotted and purple blended)	Willow, birch and poplar	Young larva in leaf shelter
Buckeye	Plaintain, stonecrops or gerardia	Larva (chrysalis)
Fritillaries	Violets, goldenrods	Chrysalis

Angle wings { Comma butterfly, Question mark }	Hops, elm and nettles	Adults
Mourning Cloak	Poplar, elm, willow and hackleberry	Adults
Cabbage butterfly	Cabbage	Pupa (chrysalis)
Swallowtails (Spicebush)	Sassafras, spicebush	Pupa (chrysalis)
Black	Parsley, carrots	Pupa (chrysalis)
Tiger	Wild cherry	Pupa (chrysalis)
Zebra	Pawpaw	Pupa (chrysalis)

MOTHS

Moth	Type of Vegetation	Winters
Acrea	Grasses and garden plants	Hibernates as larva and pupates in spring
Banded woolly bears (Isabella)	Plantain	Hibernates as larva and pupates in spring
Sphinx (Tomato or tobacco worm)	Tomato, tobacco, potatoes, birch	Pupa, in ground

(This is the worm on which wasp cocoons are often seen. Wasps lay eggs on living caterpillars.)

Ailanthus silk moth	Ailanthus	Cocoon
Cercopia	Cherry, maple, willow	Cocoon
Promethia	Sassafras, wild cherry, tulip, sweet gum	Cocoon in dry leaf on twig
Polyphemus	Oak, hickory, elm, maple, birch and other trees	Cocoon in dry leaves on ground
Io (Sharp spines are mildly poisonous. Handle with care.)	Corn and other garden and wild plants	Cocoon in dry leaf on ground
Luna (Probably most beautiful of all moths. Night flying.)	Sweet gum, walnut, hickory and persimmon	Cocoon, on ground

Imperial	Pine, hickory, oak, maple	Pupa, in ground
Corn earworm	Corn, wild plants and other garden plants	Pupa, in ground
White-marked tussock	Shade and ornamental trees	Egg
Gypsy	Shade and forest trees	Egg
Tent caterpillar	Forest, shade and ornamental trees	Egg
Cankerworm	Apple and other trees	Egg or pupa in bark
Coddling moth	Apple trees	Larva, pupates in spring
Bagworms	Cone-bearing shrubs	Pupa, sometimes in cocoon (bags of twigs)

Fun with Insects

Cricket Cage

The Japanese keep singing insects in small cages made of copper wire or small bamboo twigs. Late in the summer at the Festival of the Singing Insects the cages are opened and the insects are let free to enjoy life in the open before the frost comes.

Crickets are fun to study. Make a cricket cage of a glass jar which you keep covered with a piece of screen. Or make a cage of screen and wood. A lamp chimney placed on a pot of soil and kept covered with cheesecloth or wire screening will suffice. If the jar is over eight inches tall no top is needed as crickets cannot jump high.

Place a layer of fine sand in the bottom of the cage as crickets lay their eggs in the ground. Place a piece of decayed wood on two stones in the cage. The male will mount the wood and chirp there in broad daylight though he usually prefers to chirp at night. Keep the cage out of the sun.

A cricket makes a sound by rubbing the file on the under side of one wing against the roughened surface on the upper side. It is as if he were playing a fiddle. When he fiddles the movements are so fast that the parts making the sounds are a blur. Watch a cricket through a hand lens and see if you can see how the sound is made.

When the cricket is not using his fiddle he folds it snugly down over his back as a protective covering for his wings.

Crickets are the harbingers of spring. Theirs is the first insect chorus of spring and the last in the fall. They chirp faster at high temperatures.

Crickets make interesting pets, but keep them caged as they can do damage to clothing and carpets. Feed them lettuce and bits of moist bread, melon rind, apples and bananas. The Chinese keep several hundred crickets in one room to enjoy their chirping. Sometimes the Chinese owner will brush paraffin wax on the fiddle with a tiny brush to improve the music.

You will want field crickets for your cage. Try to get both a female (has a long spike ovipositor which sticks out behind) and a male. Crickets do not have a pupa stage and the larva does not differ much from an adult. Look for crickets in warm weather under stones, logs or in the debris of a roadside dump. They like to hide under objects. To catch them, turn an object over quickly and be ready for a fast move with a net.

Fun with Clouds and Stars

Cloud Study

Clouds belong to everybody, city and country dweller alike. To the meteorologist, sailor or fisherman the study of clouds is important in predicting the weather. The artist sees the beauty of the clouds, the natural history student combines many interests in his study of clouds. Aviators, too, must study clouds.

Since all of us are a combination of artist, weather predictor, natural scientist, fisherman or sailor, we can appreciate and study the clouds from every standpoint. Grandma may help the family weather predictions along by announcing a change in the weather as indicated either by her corns or arthritis. With that help and a look at the clouds we can arrive at a fairly accurate prediction and then check with the radio weather report to substantiate our guess. Like the sailors we often repeat to ourselves: "A red sky at night is a sailor's

delight. A red sky in the morning is a sailor's warning." As children
and adults (if we have not let ourselves grow too old) we often
see cloud pictures in the sky. Look there! See that large bear chasing
that little one. Oh! Wish we had a spoon long enough to dip into that
gigantic bowlful of vanilla ice cream there.

We all thrill to a magnificent sunset. Most of us react unhappily
to a prolonged period of dull gray days, our tempers flare oftener,
we feel depressed. When the sun comes out again and skies turn
blue, our dispositions grow sunny again with the pleasant weather.

We notice with interest a ring around the moon. When we see a
ring around the sun we grow excited. If we aren't scientists enough
to understand why the sun has a ring, we and hundreds like us flood
the switchboards of the newspapers or natural history museums to
learn the reason for its presence there.

When the cloud formation is just right, we see radiating lines coming from the horizon and pointing to the sun. As children we always
said this was the sun drawing the water from the earth to the sky.
While this process goes on invisibly every day, it is never so dramati-
cally demonstrated as it is then. We sometimes find ourselves singing
"Look for the Silver Lining" when we see one in a cumulus cloud.
We react in many ways to clouds, yet few of us could give a simple
answer to the question: "What is a cloud?"

A cloud is simply any visible mass of tiny droplets of water or
minute particles of ice suspended in the air. At home we often create
a cloud of steam when we allow our teakettle to boil. The water in
the kettle when heated vaporizes and pours out of the spout into the
cooler mass of air above the kettle. In winter, when we blow the
warm moist air from our mouths out into the surrounding cold air
we make a little cloud. When this vapor either from the kettle or
our mouths hits a cold surface, it condenses into droplets of water
and steams it up. The windows in our houses steam up or become
covered with little droplets of water. The car windows fog over when
we get into a cold car and exhale a lot of warm moist air which condenses on the windshield and windows.

The earth is surrounded by layers of air. During the day the sun draws water from the rivers, lakes, oceans and any moist surface on the earth by the process of evaporation in which the earth releases its moisture in the form of vapor. When the rising vapor reaches a layer of cool air, the moisture condenses into tiny droplets of water on microscopic bits of dust particles in the atmosphere and becomes suspended in the air in the form of clouds. When darkness falls some of the moisture returns to the earth in the form of dew or frost if the air is cool enough.

The cloud classification used today was adopted by the International Meteorological Commission in 1929. It is based on Luke Howard's classification of 1803. Howard classified the three types as cirrus or cat's-tail, stratus or high fog and cumulus or heaped. Today's main classifications are: high clouds—cirrus, cirro-stratus and cirro-cumulus, 20,000 feet and above; middle clouds—alto-cumulus and alto-stratus, 6,500 to 20,000 feet; low clouds—strato-cumulus, stratus and nimbo-stratus, near ground level to 6,500 feet; and vertical clouds, those having vertical development from 1,600 to over 20,000 feet—cumulus and cumulus-nimbus.

A brief description of the characteristics of each follows to help you identify each.

HIGH CLOUDS

Cirrus Clouds (Cat's-Tail, Feather Clouds or Curl Clouds)
Formed: Usually at high altitudes where temperature is below the freezing point, 20,000-30,000 feet
Formation: Minute ice particles
Color: Whitish generally
Characteristics: Feathery, fibrous like a tangled web, fleecy, filmy, sometimes curling, sometimes radiating in the formation of a fan Cirrus clouds are semitransparent and do not cast shadows on the earth.
Cirro-Stratus
Thin, delicate, tangled web type usually about 32,000 feet. Often arranged in layers or sheets. Gives sky a milky appear-

ance. May cause a halo, called a cirro-nebula around the sun or moon.

Cirro-Cumulus

Height about 27,000 feet, small fleecy balls arranged in groups or rows. It is this formation which is called a mackerel sky.

MIDDLE CLOUDS

Alto-Cumulus

Layer of flattened round masses in lines or groups, so close that the masses sometimes overlap each other

Alto-Stratus

Bluish or gray clouds in sheetlike formation. They resemble cirro-stratus but are lower and heavier and are without halo phenomena. A gray veil-like formation which sometimes hides the sun or moon partially or completely.

LOW CLOUDS

Stratus

Formed: Low levels

Color: Gray

Characteristics: Resembles fog, but does not rest on the ground. Usually arranged parallel to the ground in layers or bands. This is the gray-skies cloud that covers the earth for days at a time and obscures the sun. Wisps of stratus may be so low they blot out tops of tall buildings.

Strato-Cumulus

Thick and sometimes overlapping ball-shaped forms of stratus are given this name. These usually appear in winter and are soft gray or darker in color.

Nimbo-Stratus

This is the snow or rain cloud. It is a layer of uniformly dark gray cloud which usually produces continuous rain or snow which falls from its ragged lower edge.

VERTICAL CLOUDS

Cumulus

Formed: In the lower part of the atmosphere at the level at which water vapor begins to condense into droplets of water
Formation: Minute droplets of liquid water
Color: Snowy white. May appear dark when the sun is behind them. With the sun behind them they appear to have a silver lining.
Characteristics: A flat-based formation of lumpy, rounded domes piled high on each other. They sail across the sky on a windy day like huge cotton-ball ships. These are the fair weather clouds.
Since they are dense masses, they cast a shadow on the earth that will run ahead of your car or cross its path as you drive along. This is the cloud that forms the dramatic backdrop for the demonsration of how the sun draws the moisture from the earth.

THUNDER CLOUD

Cumulo-Nimbus

This is a cumulus cloud charged with electricity that produces lightning and thunder. A cumulus of great vertical development that rises high into the atmosphere becomes the thunder cloud, the most dramatic and exciting cloud formation of all.

Cloud Facts

Clouds are found more often over the ocean than over land and seldom over desert regions. Along the coast of an ocean with its oceanic winds, clouds will be found in abundance.

Clouds are wind-propelled and move in the direction of the wind. In winter clouds move faster since they are lower in the atmosphere and because winter winds are stronger. High light cirrus clouds may move as fast as 250 miles per hour.

Make a Cloud Mirror

To study clouds from a comfortable position without danger of eye strain, paint one side of a piece of glass with black enamel or lacquer. Lay it on the ground or watch the cloud reflections move across your cloud mirror. Watch one form change into another. Try to estimate how fast they are moving. Check with your airport weather station on wind speeds and see how close your guess is.

Cloud Photography

The camera fiends in families will have fun trying to capture and preserve on black and white or color film the beautiful and dramatic cloud formations: the thunderheads, the sunsets and sunrises, the mackerel sky formations, the lump clouds with the silver lining and even the flashes of lightning of the thunderclouds. The patient photographer may even catch lightning striking a high building if he keeps his camera focused and ready during an electrical storm.

Those working with color film may prepare a whole series of cloud slides showing each type in various settings—in cities with tall buildings as backgrounds, in the mountains, at the seashore or in the country with rolling hills and wooded slopes.

Clouds and Weather Reports

Cloudiness is one of the elements of climate. The proportion of the sky covered by any form of cloud determines the weather report. For example:

"Clear weather" is reported when the sky is less than three-tenths covered with clouds.

"Partly cloudy" is reported when the sky is three- to seven-tenths clouds.

More than seven-tenths is "cloudy."

"Cloudless" is the fair weather extreme and "overcast" is the opposite extreme.

The United States averages about 50 per cent cloudiness. The areas having the least cloudy weather are Arizona and adjacent Southwest areas. The Great Lakes regions and the Washington and Oregon coast have the most—60–70 per cent.

Astronomy

Each person should be able to identify at least ten major constellations, know the difference between a planet and a star, be able to locate some of the brightest stars. Whether we live in the city or country, in the North or South, the stars are above us. Study with field glasses or a small telescope makes the stars even more fascinating.

Star books are available at your bookstores or ten-cent stores. If your city has a natural history museum with a planetarium don't fail to pay it a visit several times a year. If your city does not have such a facility, make it a point to visit one when you are on vacation in another city.

Some facts which should help you in developing an interest in stars follow. A plan for making a simple planetarium is given later in this chapter.

Star Facts

A star is a heavenly body which shines by its own light rather than by reflected light. Each star is a body similar to the sun.

Planets, satellites and moons shine in the sky but reflect the light of a star or sun.

Stars are farther away from the earth than the sun and are vastly larger. Our sun which is 860,000 miles in diameter is about average as stars go.

The sun is 93,000,000 miles away from the earth. The closest star, Alpha Centauri (found in the Southern sky) is 25,000,000,-000,000 miles away. Since light travels at the rate of 186,000 miles per second, it takes the light of Alpha Centauri more than four years to reach the earth.

Stars were originally divided into six classes, the brightest being designated as first magnitude and those just visible to the naked eye as sixth magnitude. First magnitude stars are one hundred times brighter than sixth magnitude stars. Those brighter than first magnitude are designated by minus number.

About six thousand stars are visible to the naked eye. The number visible with powerful telescopes is around 500,000,000. It has been estimated that there are about four billion stars. The Palomar telescope can photograph stars six million times fainter than those we can see with the naked eye.

The filmy band which crosses the heavens is known as the Milky Way. It is a huge irregular circle of stars. It is brightest in Sagittarius.

Because people thought that the stars outlined different forms, they gave them names of persons in their myths and legends. Most of the names come from Greek and Roman mythology. The brighter stars such as Sirius and Arcturus have their own names. Some are designated by letters in the Greek alphabet or by numbers.

There are double, triple and quadruple stars. Over a third of the stars are double or "binary." Some can be seen without a telescope. The star at the curve of the Big Dipper (Mizar) is a double star and can be seen on a clear night. Binary stars revolve around the same center of gravity. One may eclipse the other as they revolve and the brightness of the star waxes and wanes. Algol, in Perseus, waxes and wanes at intervals of three days. The binaries may be as far apart as thirteen million miles, yet to us they appear close enough to be double!

Star clusters are group of stars having common characteristics. If the stars in a group are about the same distance from the earth, move in the same direction at the same rate of speed but are widely scattered they are called a galactic cluster. This type appears in the Milky Way chiefly. A small compact cluster of stars is called a globular cluster. The Pleiades and the cluster in Orion are globular clusters and are visible to the naked eye.

Stars twinkle, planets do not. The light of the stars is refracted as it passes through the earth's atmosphere which causes the twinkling effect. Planets which are of relatively larger size do not twinkle except when they are low in the sky.

Stars are in motion but the motion is so slight in the course of one lifetime the movement would not be noticed unless one studied a particular star and observed it constantly over a period of many years. Because the movement is so imperceptible the stars are called fixed stars. Planets which revolve around our sun as the earth does appear in different locations in the sky at different times of the year.

The Circumpolar Constellations

If you are viewing the heavens from somewhere between the North Pole and the Equator, the stars near the Pole are always in view. Because the earth turns on its axis, these constellations seem to wheel in the sky. At forty degrees latitude they never set. In Florida which is in the thirtieth parallel, these constellations set and are therefore no longer circumpolar.

The circumpolar constellations are the best to begin your star study with. They are easily located and will serve as guides to other constellations.

The map given here shows the location of these, the five key con-

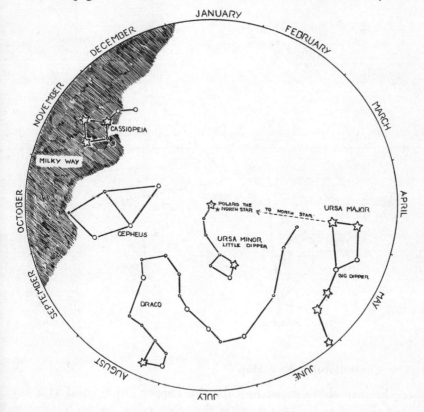

stellations. To use the map, face north. Turn the sky map until the current month is at top. This will give you the correct location at 9:00 P.M. in that month. If you are viewing it at a later hour, turn the map counterclockwise; for an earlier time turn it clockwise. A quarter turn in either direction will show the difference in position in a six-hour period.

The best time to begin study is early in the evening before the sky is too dark and filled with too many stars. The brighter stars show first in the evening sky.

The Constellations Key Map

The map above shows how the Big Dipper can be used as a key constellation in locating some of the other constellations. Consult a star map which will give you the locations for the current month of the particular constellations you wish to study. Then use this key map and you are ready to go. Binoculars will make the study of each particular star more fun. When you are thoroughly familiar with a few constellations visit an observatory when it is open to the public and see the stars through a telescope. A whole wonderful new world is open to you in star study.

Home Planetarium

To make a simple home planetarium which will help you to recognize constellations more readily proceed in this manner:

1. Take a tin can and cut top and bottom lids out with your can opener.

2. In the center of a piece of typing paper draw a circle the size of the opening in the can. You can use the can as a pattern.

3. Within the confines of this circle draw the circumpolar constellations using a good star map as a guide.

4. With a pin prick the positions of the stars making the holes big enough so that light can shine through them.

5. Stretch this star map tightly over one open end of the tin can. A rubber band will hold it in place securely.

6. Use your biggest flashlight and hold it in the other end of the can so that the light will shine on the star map.

7. Darken the room and project your star map on a blank wall or a sheet of white paper. Move back and forth until you have a good clear focus.

8. Study this map until you can recognize the constellations without referring to your star map. Then go out and try to find these same constellations in the heavens.

9. Make a new map as soon as you have learned the constellations on the first.

NATURE HOBBIES—THE DOORS TO WONDERLAND

A child's interest in his world can be fostered and stimulated in his home at an early age. Family excursions to seashore, fields or woods are not only fun but educational. Parents who expose their children to opportunities for learning more about their world open doors to a wonderland that never loses appeal.

Parents who make such opportunities available to their children often find hobbies and interests for themselves. It has happened more than once in a natural history museum after a family visit that Junior comes back to join a class for children. Father in bringing him discovers the class in gem cutting or telescope making is one he simply cannot pass up.

It is natural for children to watch with pleasure clouds moving across the sky. They ask the questions of children everywhere: "What is a cloud? What is wind? Where is it going?" It is natural for children to press their whys, whats, hows and wheres until they get answers that satisfy them. Some are quieted with the simplest answer. "What is that noise, Mother?" asks one with eyes wide with wonder. "That is a bluejay scolding a squirrel, darling," the mother answers. One child will be satisfied with that answer. Another will be challenged to search further. "What is a bluejay? Why is it quarreling with the squirrel? Can they understand each other?"

When a child not only sees and hears the things about him but begins to question—at that moment a student of nature is born. If he does not get his answers at home he will seek them at the library or museum.

One child may never get beyond the beginner level. Another will continue to ask questions and seek answers for the rest of his life, filling his leisure time with the search, advancing from beginner to advanced student-naturalist to amateur explorer-naturalist. Another will fill his entire life with his study and become a trained scientist. Whether he delves deeply or is content with what he learns after a casual search, that individual will have an avocation that will bring him pleasure and enjoyment all his years. With each season and in every new place he visits, the picture is one that is constantly changing, is always new and filled with fascinating facts.

If he never leaves his home town, possibilities for unlimited adventures with Nature lie within his reach. If all he does is to discover for himself what others have learned before him, the thrill is still there. A child who studies a star map and then finds in reality the constellation he has seen a moment before on a piece of paper becomes as excited as if he had been the first to discover it. *Seeing* something for the first time after merely *looking* at it for years is a thrilling experience.

The greater his knowledge, the more he sees. Even then, until he knows the facts, he cannot be sure that things are as they seem. Is water really blue or is it merely reflecting the blue of the sky? When can he trust his eyes? When can he not? He sees a bird alight on the ground near him. He does not see it fly away again. But look as he will, he no longer sees it. Protective coloring allows the bird to lose itself in the background. If he believes his eyes, he walks away telling himself nothing is there. If he knows about protective coloring he no longer trusts his eyes alone. He advances carefully and quietly. His reward is to see the almost invisible bird hiding there practically at his feet.

One time he may flush up a bird in his walk through the fields. It flutters away from him frightened and apparently hurt. Perhaps it has an injured wing. Maybe he can catch it and give it aid. It seems to be asking him to catch it. But is it? If he knows about the bird, he realizes it is putting on a show to draw his attention, Mamma is not hurt. She's just carrying on a diversionary campaign to focus his attention on her and away from her vulnerable babies. If he gets too close to her she flies off.

So—if the child never gets beyond the nature interest stage, he will have fun with nature all his life. If he goes on to the beginner-student level, he will still be able to enjoy all the aspects of nature that delight his senses. He will have the fun of working out some of the riddles that confront him each day. Each step forward increases his possibilities for enjoyment.

If he wishes to go further and work for the good of others, he can as a trained amateur observe, record and accumulate the facts that will help to fill in the blanks and add to man's store of knowledge. The trained scientists are busy with the important tasks of naming and classifying the species, or laying down other necessary and important foundations of facts. But they build only a foundation. Upon it must be built the structure of many facts compiled by amateurs and scientists during hours of painstaking and careful observations.

If he would be pioneer, explorer, experimenter or adventurer, he can be so with a nature hobby. It may be your child or the corner storekeeper who never went further than a hundred miles from home who will discover how to prevent the chestnut blight, how a cat purrs or the life cycle of a particular insect. In so doing he may fill in one of the blanks and make his mark upon the history of the natural sciences as did the famous amateurs Audubon, Fabre and Thoreau and countless others.

Of all the opportunities for family play, nature hobbies are the most satisfying, fascinating, most accessible for nature is all around us. We can bring it into our homes in aquariums, terrariums or in pots of earth. We can tame a bird and bring its song into our living room. We can watch the miracle of life being enacted under our very eyes. We can, in fact, help a miracle along with our own hands as we break off a leaf and put it in a container of water to root and begin life anew. We can watch the skies from our windows and make our own weather predictions. We can do these things alone as individuals or together as families. Every period of the day has its phenomena, each season its treats and surprises. Weather cannot often spoil a proposed excursion for weather itself is one of the fields of study. The price of the tickets to the wonderland of adventure is humbleness and a realization of our own vast ignorance and an insatiable curiosity. All we do helps us to learn about our own world of which we are an insignificant yet important part.

10

Family Parties

Family parties are probably the most fun of all. They do not necessarily involve members of one family only but may include several families of friends or relatives. They may center around family anniversaries such as birthdays or wedding anniversaries or around certain holidays such as Thanksgiving, Christmas or New Year's Eve. They may be just-for-fun parties given for no reason other than that parties are fun.

Family Birthday Celebrations

Celebrating on the actual day is often more important to children than to adults, who eventually reach the time when birthdays seem better forgotten than celebrated. Sometimes the actual day is not the best day for the celebration because all members of the family cannot be at home. The celebration is then moved up to the closest Sunday when more members can conveniently be present. Sometimes if a number of birthdays come within a period of a few weeks a joint celebration is held. The singing of the happy birthday song becomes a rather confused rendition when each birthday celebrant sings "Happy birthday to me" while the other members of the family try to get in all the names of the birthdayites in one mad scramble before the music gives out. The presentation of gifts and the ensuing unwrapping session when several birthdays are celebrated at the same time is as much fun as Christmas especially if some of the gifts are joke gifts.

It is more fun at a child's party if the gifts are not just placed on the table. The child is given a treasure hunt route to follow which leads to the cache of birthday gifts.

Birthday cakes with fortunes baked in them add to the fun of the occasion. Small tokens such as a shiny new dime, a ten-cent store diamond ring, and other small metal items contribute more to the lightness of the occasion than to the cake. They can be purchased at any ten-cent store counter which sells novelties and supplies for parties. One word of caution—warn the cake eaters they may be striking treasures. A tooth broken on one of the hidden items can make treasure hunting disastrous.

Thanksgiving Day Celebration

Some families like to keep this day for the immediate family members only. Others invite friends whose families are far away or foreign students who would find this vacation time a lonely period and feel themselves well rewarded for their concern for others. The day becomes more than an occasion to stuff oneself to the gills. It becomes a day for sharing ideas and experiences.

If a program is planned for part of the day, Thanksgiving becomes a very special occasion. A session of singing or a program of colored slides taken on a recent trip by one of the persons present makes the day an even more memorable one.

When families thus open their hearts as well as their homes to friends and strangers who might otherwise spend a lonely day they find that their family celebration has suffered in no way and has, in fact, been enhanced.

Little Surprise Parties

Little surprise parties sometimes are the best fun of all because they come completely as a surprise as they are extemporaneously planned. Any member of the family may get an idea and without giving a bit of warning retire to the kitchen and prepare a special treat for everybody. At dinner some night, Dad or an older brother may suddenly distribute surprise gifts for everybody.

Little parties may be held to celebrate an especially nice occurrence

such as getting on the honor roll, getting a new job or a salary increase or whatever. They may be held because everyone's morale seems to be at low ebb and needs a booster shot which a little party most certainly gives. Actually there need be no special occasion or excuse for springing a little party except that they are fun for everybody.

Snow Ice Cream

Snow ice cream is enough of an unexpected surprise to make a little party. For example there has been a fresh snowfall. Clean snow is everywhere. Mom gathers up a large bowlful and mixes it with sweetened whipping cream flavored with vanilla until it is a sherbert-like mixture. It is a surprisingly good treat.

Jack Wax Treat

Areas which have maple sugar bushes will know about jack wax, others may not. In sugar bush country, clean snow is placed on individual platters or plates. Maple syrup is boiled until it is thick and stringy. The hot syrup is then poured on the snow in script style, writing the person's name with the hot syrup (jack wax) on the snow. The syrup hardens and makes good, sticky, chewy eating which is all the more fun since the way of serving it is novel.

Coasting Parties

It's a winter Saturday morning or Sunday afternoon. Snow has been falling for the past few hours. The ground is well covered. Suddenly Dad announces: "Okay, kids, put on your snow things and get out your sleds. We're going over to the coasting hill for some old-fashioned belly slamming." Never do the kids respond to an order more quickly or willingly. Some of the neighborhood kids are rounded up with a few quick phone calls. In no time at all a carful of people is off to the hills. No one needs to be urged to clean up his plate at mealtime following that session. The food disappears like the proverbial snowball on the Fourth of July.

Finger Painting Party

Mom prepares for this one a long time ahead and keeps her counsel until the propitious time arrives. Comes a day when the family seems to be needing a dose of a little party. The dining room table is opened to its largest size and covered with a thick layer of protective newspapers. Out come the jars of finger paints and many sheets of finger painting paper. Everyone gets in the act. The various colored paints are set in the middle of the table, each with its plastic spoon or tongue depressor ladle. A pan of clean water is placed in the center of the table with a clean cellulose sponge. Everyone takes his place at the table, each selects the color he wants and soon everyone is merrily creating with one or both hands. The first masterpieces are soon finished. These are laid to dry on newspapers placed on the floor to protect the rugs. Someone gets the idea of putting a certain selection on the record player to see what music will do for the artists. It surprises everyone how much fun it is to paint to the rhythm of the music. It isn't always the adults who turn out the most beautiful or interesting painting either, which makes this kind of surprise more fun than anything.

Taffy Pulls

Taffy pulls need not be old-fashioned treats of the past. People love candy now just as much as they did in years past. Pulling the taffy can be just as much fun. With a good candy thermometer, a recipe, and with all the family in on the pull, this makes a good little party treat.

TAFFY RECIPE

Boil together:

> 1 cup molasses
> 2 teaspoons vinegar
> ¾ cup sugar

When mixture reaches 265–270 degrees on candy thermometer add:

> 1 tablespoon butter
> ⅛ teaspoon baking soda
> ⅛ teaspoon salt

Add favorite flavoring. Color with food color if you wish. Stir only until blended. Pour into a well-buttered pan. Allow to cool just until cool enough to handle. Pull with buttered hands until porous.

Cut with buttered scissors or sharp knife into one-inch pieces.

Caramel Corn Treat

It's been a long hard winter, everyone feels a bit low. All of a sudden a delicious smell begins coming from the kitchen. Sniff, sniff, what's going on? Smells like popcorn and something else too. Gradually the curious gravitate toward the kitchen. A surprise is in the making. Mom is popping corn on one burner and has something cooking on the other.

"Go away," she says. "I'll let you know when it's ready." Who wants to go away? Things certainly are more interesting out here than they are in the living room. Soon the mystery mixture on the stove is ready and is poured over the freshly popped corn. Yum, Yum! Caramel corn is a yummy concoction. Boredom? Low spirits? They vanish with the first bite. There's nothing like a surprise to liven things up especially when it tastes as good as this one.

CARAMEL CORN RECIPE

Mix together:

1 cup brown sugar
1¼ cup molasses
1 cup water
8 teaspoons vinegar
¼ teaspoon cream of tartar

Boil to the hard ball stage or 250 degrees on your candy thermometer.
Add 3 teaspoons soda.
Flavor with 2 teaspoons vanilla.
The mixture will foam up a bit. Pour over two large bowlfuls of freshly popped corn mixed with salted nuts. This will make enough for a large family and feed the neighbors' children as well.

"Read a Story" Party

This is one of the most fun of all little parties. Mom or Dad suddenly announces that the entertainment of the evening will be a surprise story party. Everyone gets into comfortable lounging clothes. Each finds his most comfortable position on the davenport, floor or chair. When everybody is nicely settled, Mom or Dad begins the reading session. Who ever gets too old to enjoy a story? How many times can you listen to an old favorite without tiring? Who fails to thrill to the first reading of a new story? Try this kind of little party and learn the answers.

What to read? Begin with old favorites. Ask your librarian for suggestions of books which make good reading aloud. A few books are suggested below:

FAMILY RECREATIONAL READING SUGGESTIONS

Borland, H. G., *High, Wide and Lonesome.* Lippincott, 1956.
Bowie, Walter Russell, *Bible Stories for Boys and Girls, New Testament.* Abingdon-Cokesbury Press, 1952.

Bowie, Walter Russell, *Bible Stories for Boys and Girls, Old Testament.* Abingdon-Cokesbury Press, 1951.
Chute, Marchette, *The Innocent Wayfaring.* Scribner's, 1943.
Crile, Jane, *Treasure-Diving Holidays.* Viking Press, 1954.
Durrell, Gerald M., *The Drunken Forest.* Viking Press, 1954.
Forbes, Kathryn (pseud.), *Mama's Bank Account.* Harcourt, Brace, 1943.
Gilbreth, F. B., *Cheaper by the Dozen.* Crowell, 1948.
Heyerdahl, Thor, *Kon-Tiki.* Rand McNally, 1950.
Moody, Ralph, *Little Britches.* Norton, 1950.
Mowat, Farley, *The Dog Who Wouldn't Be.* Little, Brown, 1957.
Papashvily, Helen and George, *Anything Can Happen.* Harper & Brothers, 1945.
Papashvily, Helen and George, *Yes and No Stories.* Harper & Brothers, 1946.
Papashvily, Helen and George, *Thanks to Noah.* Harper & Brothers, 1951.
Street, James, *Goodbye, My Lady.* Lippincott, 1954.
Twain, Mark (pseud.), *The Adventures of Mark Twain.* World, 1937.
Ullman, J. R., *Banner in the Sky.* Lippincott, 1954.
Walker, David Harry, *Geordie.* Houghton Mifflin, 1950.
Werner, Jane, *Bible Stories of Boys and Girls.* Simon & Schuster, 1953.
West, Jessamyn, *Cress Delahanty.* Harcourt, Brace, 1953.
Wibberly, Leonard, *McGillicuddy McGotham.* Little, Brown, 1956.

"Play-a-Game" Little Party

Comes a time when everyone has that what'll-we-do feeling which tends to make people act a bit peevish. This is a good time to pull out the Parchesi board or a new game which Mom has bought and hidden away for just such an occasion. The family gathers around the dining table and plays a game together. The kind of game in which every member of the family except baby can participate is the best. Play your family favorite or try out a new game. A special snack treat following the game completes the cure.

"Try-a-Stunt" Little Party

Stunts work at any kind of family gathering or party. They are fun at little parties. The stunts given below are called "resolution of forces" stunts. Any one of them will give a lift to a party.

The trick of these stunts is to do them seriously. The trouble is that at the most solemn moment someone explodes with laughter or gives an out-of-control snort of glee and the whole group collapses. Time-out has to be called until everyone can straighten his face and pull himself together so the show can go on.

These stunts prove that when there is concerted effort something that was impossible to do before becomes possible if all stunters concentrate and co-operate. Try those stunts sometimes when there is a heavy piece of furniture to move and see for yourselves how useful the application of this principle can be. Several types are given here.

HANDS ON HEAD STUNT

One person sits on a straight chair. Four persons group themselves around this volunteer, one at each shoulder, one at each knee. To show that there is a difference if they concentrate, the four persons place their hands under the knees and under the arms of the seated person and attempt to lift him high in the air. It is difficult to do. Now comes the concentration part. The four persons pile their hands on top of the head of the person, alternating hands as they place them. When all hands are in place, they press down lightly and count to ten. Immediately after the count of ten, they quickly put their hands under each arm and each knee and lift quickly. Almost miraculously the seated person is lifted high into the air and then lowered to the chair again. Resolution of forces makes him seem as light as a ping-pong ball and he seems almost to float into the air. Try this with four women attempting to lift a heavy man or with four children attempting to lift one of the adults. It really works! Be sure they put the person back on the chair before they decide to laugh!

KOWTOW PICK-UP

The position of the person is the same as in the stunt given above. This time, however, the lifters stand back a bit from the seated person and raise their hands high over their heads. At a signal they kowtow three times toward the seated person and after the third time place their hands under the arm and knees of the person on the chair and lift him. He floats through the air with the greatest of ease. Just be sure to warn the lifters to put the victim down before they begin to laugh or he comes down with a jolting thud and that is no fun for him!

BREATHE AND FINGER LIFT STUNT

The lifters stand in the same positions as in the previously described stunts. This time each clasps his hands together tightly allowing only the forefingers to remain extended. The seated person is to be lifted with two fingers this time! Well, actually eight fingers as there are four persons doing the lifting. Let the four practice clasping their hands and placing their extended forefingers under the knees and arms of the seated person and lifting him. Impossible? Not if there is resolution of forces. This is achieved by concentrated breathing. The four lifters stand by the seated person in their appointed places. At a signal they take three deep breaths together, inhaling and exhaling at the same time. They hold the third breath and immediately lift the seated person high into the air and put him down before they expel their breaths. This stunt tends to get a bit silly as four persons attempting to breathe together inevitably begin to snort. The process must then begin all over after everyone gets control again. The audience is no help either. One giggle from that direction and the stunt collapses.

HUMAN OUIJA STUNT

One person volunteers as the victim. The others make a circle around him standing one behind the other with their left hands resting lightly on the shoulder of the victim and their right hands resting on the shoulder of the person ahead. The victim closes his eyes and relaxes agreeing to yield to the impulse transmitted by the combined will of the group. When the eyes of the victim are closed the leader points in the direction the victim is to lean. The whole group concentrates and watches the victim. Sure enough, he begins to lean in the proper direction with only their hands on the shoulders to keep him from falling. It is a weird sensation. Actually the players without realizing it tend to lean a bit in the direction they wish the victim to go and let up pressure on the other side so he has no choice but to lean in the proper direction. Warn the group not to do any pushing but to rest their hands lightly on the victim's shoulders and will him to move in the proper direction by thought concentration.

Surprise Winter Home Picnic Little Party

Picnics are always fun, but when they come in the middle of winter right at your own dinner table they are a welcome surprise. Mom decides that it is time the family had a special surprise treat. Dinner is served picnic style on paper plates with the menu consisting of all the family picnic favorites. Broiled hamburgers or wieners, hot or cold potato salad, baked beans, pickles, soft drinks or chocolate milk for the kids and, as a special dessert, marshmallows sprinkled with coconut and placed on a salted cracker and toasted under the broiler. Just the idea of having a picnic in February makes the whole idea fun but the serving of favorite picnic food makes it taste good too.

Snowman Little Party

The snow has to be just right to make snowmen so this kind of little party can be held only when the right conditions exist. In a way this is a drop-of-the-hat party. The snow conditions are right and everyone drops anything unimportant he is doing and dresses for the occasion. Out they go and begin the business of rolling various-sized snowballs and piling them up into snowmen and ladies and animals. Old hats, whisk brooms for noses, sticks for guns, something red for lips and something for eyes are gathered up and behold—a whole family of snowpeople occupies the back or front yard!

All effort is concentrated toward this purpose except at times when the snow sculptors slyly take time out to make small snow missiles and fire them at unsuspecting victims aiming, of course, at those parts of the anatomy where a direct hit can't possibly prove fatal. If a few faces get washed and snow angels appear all over the snow (where children or adults have lain down and made their arms go like wings until an angel design is pressed into the snow) there is no harm done.

Time out for a couple of rounds of Fox and Geese, that old loved snow tag game, won't hurt anyone either. To play this game, a large circle is made in the snow by tromping the snow down. The big pie is cut in half with one line and in quarters with a second line which runs at right angles to the first. One person is designated IT. He attempts to catch any of the other players who to escape being captured can run only on the lines of the circle or the cuts in the pie. He who gets caught become IT and the chase is renewed. If the adults play they will make a big goal in the center of the circle where they are safe from capture. They will probably spend most of the game standing close enough to this safe place so that one hurried leap will render them immune to capture.

Winter Picnic

One of the most exciting of any surprise family little parties is the winter walk in the woods just after a heavy snowfall. When you walk over familiar paths now almost unrecognizable under their snowy covering; when the seedling trees and low undergrowth take on almost human appearances in their snowy dresses; when the log barriers which mark the boundaries of the summer parking lots are huge snowy-white mushrooms and the picnic tables are enormous snowy loaves of fresh bread; when yours are the first human tracks to be made along the trails in the now almost deserted park, and your voices the only human sounds to be heard in an area which in summer is a bedlam of sounds and cries of picnickers; you experience a thrill that comes only at rare instances in a lifetime.

The woods are excitingly different in the winter. The trees are naked except for a few oaks which wear tattered, ragged dresses of dried-up reddish-brown leaves. Only the evergreens are fully clothed. For the first time we can see the beauty of the patterns made by the tree trunks and their branches and notice how the bark of the various trees varies in color. The picnic grounds which hum with human noises in the summer are quiet now until we listen closely. Then sound after sound makes itself heard. From there comes the rustle of the dry leaves, here is the creak of a tall tree as it sways gently in the wind. The little stream bubbles triumphantly as it breaks free from under its covering of ice and snow. In the distance is heard the sound of an occasional car passing by on the lightly traveled park road. There is a sound of a persistent hammer where someone a half-mile away is building a house.

The cold air is bracing and stirs us into activity. With everyone warmly dressed and adequately booted, no one suffers. If at the end of the walk a roaring fire awaits with wieners and marshmallows to be toasted over its coals, and steaming mugs of hot chocolate poured from the Thermos, to warm our hands through our mittens as well as our insides, the day is complete. The adults feel the cares and tensions of the world fall away and a sense of peace wash over them. The children, too, relax and unwind under the magic spell. A winter walk in the woods after a new snow is a memorable occasion to be treasured as one of the highlights of family fun experiences.

Make Your Own Little Party

Each family has its favorite activities. Use these as a basis for making a surprise little party. It may involve having some favorite person appear unexpectedly at dinner some night. It may be a sudden announcement that if enough people are ready and willing, a trip to the zoo is in order with the family bus scheduled to leave the home terminal in thirty minutes flat. All who are going better be ready with clean faces, fresh shirts, etc., etc. It may be a trip to a roller rink on a Sunday afternoon when family groups are invited to skate together or a trip to an ice-skating pond or indoor ice rink. Whatever the activity, whenever it is held, the little parties will be some of the highlights of happy family memories because they were the times the family played together. There are no happier memories than these.

I I

Family Picnics and Cook-outs

Picnic is a word full of wonderful fun connotations. It means many
things to different people. Just the mention of the word makes people's faces light up. The word is often used to describe an especially
happy occasion so to say, "We had a picnic" is to give it the highest
possible praise.

For most people, a picnic means certain tasty foods, an excursion
in the family car to a favorite park or picnicking area, eating outside
and wide-open spaces for the kids to romp in. As a family activity, a
picnic is a natural because there is something for every member of the
family to enjoy and a good piece of the great outdoors to enjoy it in.
A number of families can join together for the occasion without the
strain that accompanies entertaining in the home. Sometimes just the
thoughts of having a large enough table, chairs for everyone and
preparing a big meal often kills a party before it is born. The matter
of entertaining a number of children at a home party is a problem
too, which requires serious consideration. At a picnic, however, the
matter of tables and chairs is no problem. It may mean only taking
care to reserve a picnic area with sufficient facilities to handle the
crowd in mind. Entertaining the children at a park is more a matter
of occasional supervision since there may be a ball field, wading area,
playground and nature trails to keep them busy and happy. The
"What'll we do?" question at a picnic is easily answered. One can
be as active as one wants to or just sit around the table and "chew the
fat" or lie in a blanket under the trees and relax. Usually the worry is,

will we have enough time for all the things we want to do rather than, what can we do?

Whether we are considering a picnic for our own family or organizing one with other families, a plan is necessary. Too often the burden of planning and preparing the picnic lunch is left entirely to Mom. A family council should be called when a picnic is planned. The picnic location can be voted on or left to Dad who may have a surprise place in mind. The menu can be the result of family planning with each member taking on some responsibility for making or helping to prepare some part of the food. The duties of packing the car at home, unpacking at the picnic area, repacking to come back home and the final clean-up at home should be assigned to various members of the family so that all the burden does not fall on Mom or Dad. The children should understand that there will be more family picnics if everyone does his share in the work aspects of the affair. Children can be taught at an early age that fun has its accompanying responsibilities. If everyone helps, much of the work is taken out of the family excursion and all the fun is left in.

Have a Work Plan

Plan the work activities and divide them into projects. The young children can be assigned the simplest tasks. The other work projects are written on pieces of paper and drawn by the various members. Work assignments then become a matter of chance and not parent's choice. This plan eliminates the cry of "I always get stuck with the dirty jobs." Each participant understands his responsibilities and knows exactly what is expected of him.

Mom needs help in the kitchen preparing the food. The children too young to cook can help with some of the preparation. Scraping carrots, washing celery, icing the cake, buttering the bread for sandwiches or cutting up the vegetables for the potato salad are some of the jobs the children can do. Dad will need help filling the car icebox with ice cubes, milk and soft drinks and with packing the car.

Family Picnic Kit

A family which owns a picnic kit that is always kept replenished and in readiness can plan a picnic at the drop of a suggestion. All that has to be prepared is the food and "they're off" to the park.

Make Your Own Picnic Kit

The kit can be a cardboard box with a tight cover or a clean lined bushel basket. The type of liner sold in supermarkets or variety stores as a laundry basket liner is ideal and inexpensive. A bushel basket is easy to obtain from your favorite grocer. Ask for the woven lid that came with it. Since the basket has two handles, it is easily carried by two children or one adult. Such a basket costs nothing, is readily obtainable, is spacious and is easily stored between picnics.

SUGGESTED PICNIC KIT CONTENTS

1. Sectional paper plates or washable reusable aluminum or plastic plates
2. Paper cups or plastic unbreakable cups

3. Stainless steel knives, forks, spoons and serving spoons

4. Small tin box for matches (Matches may be waterproofed by dipping the heads in melted paraffin.)

5. Several large salt shakers with screw lids. Some special seasonings are now sold in shakers which have a plastic lid with holes and a tin lid which screws on over the plastic cap. These would make excellent picnic basket shakers. The salt will not cake in such a container and the contents cannot spill in the basket.

6. Package of paper napkins

7. Package of paper hankies

8. Roll of toilet tissue

9. Spatula, long-handled forks, mixing spoon, sharp knife and a paring knife

10. A big frying pan, coffee pot and a kettle for heating water for dishes. These should be kept in separate plastic bags so they will not soil other things in the basket.

11. Wiener forks

12. Roll of aluminum foil

13. Airtight jar of sugar or sugar lumps and one of the nonfattening sweeteners for calorie watchers

14. A large plastic tablecloth

15. A cellulose sponge

16. Package of soapy steel wool pads

17. A plastic bag filled with soap powder or detergent for cleaning-up purposes (A can of liquid detergent is also suitable.)

18. A soap dish with a bar of hand soap, a roll of paper towels or an old hand towel, and a washbasin for washing up before meals. The basin can double as a dishpan later.

19. Small first-aid kit with bandages, band-aids, poison ivy lotion, insect repellent, sunburn lotion, antiseptic, adhesive tape and a bottle of alcohol. Include a pair of scissors, needles for slivers, a package of matches for sterilizing needles, tweezers, and a package of cotton.

20. Whisk broom or workbench brush for cleaning up picnic table and seats before and after using

21. Three or four old dish towels
22. Spray can of insect killer for spraying around and under table before using
23. Hatchet for chopping wood for fires
24. Charcoal. This can be kept in metal containers just large enough to hold a supply for one cook-out. It can be filled for each picnic. A can that contained popcorn or potato chips is a good size. Paper bags of charcoal after being opened are messy to handle and get the fire builder dirty.
25. Bundle of kindling. This can be made up at home from orange crates and apple boxes obtained at your grocery market. Tree cuttings and twigs raked from your lawn can also be used. Cut the wood into convenient lengths and wrap a supply sufficient to start one fire in several thicknesses of newspapers and tie with a cord. You will then have paper and kindling handy for fire starting. (If it is against your fire-building principles to use paper in starting a fire, you can, of course, throw the paper in the waste container after you have arrived at the picnic area and start from scratch.) Kindling bundles may be made by the children as a rainy day activity in answer to a "What can I do?" query and put aside for future reference.
26. Several old newspapers. These can be used for starting fires or to put under the tablecloth or for covering benches. They are also good for wiping up tables or benches you have washed preparatory to using.
27. One or two large grocery bags which can be used for garbage and debris. Stand one up at one end of the table. Fold back the top all around. This fold will hold the bag open at the top so garbage and other refuse can easily be put in it. The whole bag is then closed up and put in a waste container.
28. Long-handled tongs for taking things out of the fire or for turning food wrapped in foil that is cooking on the coals
29. A pair of heavy work gloves or a pair of mitt pot holders for handling hot objects and pan handles. Regular pot holders are a must, too.

30. A heavy cardboard mailing tag should be tied to the handle of the picnic kit. On one side of the tag list all the food items that are to be added at the last minute. This list would include the condiments such as catsup, mustard, horseradish, pickle relish and all relishes such as pickles, olives and other canned or bottled relishes. Coffee, tea bags, canned milk will also be on the list. (The food for the picnic is packed in another container or basket.) On the reverse side of the tag list all the items which must be replaced after each picnic. The person in charge of checking the picnic kit and filling it will then have a check list to work with. This list would include the paper items, matches, kindling, charcoal and those items which might have been used up at the last picnic.

Hints for Painless Picnics

The fact that a picnic is an outdoor affair and we are eating at a picnic table in a park does not imply that we must eat under sanitary conditions far below our normal standards for cleanliness. Eating at a dirty table in an area smelling of the garbage of a hundred previous picnics and fighting the bugs for each mouthful would cool the ardor of the most fervent picnic lover.

If the place you planned to picnic is dirty beyond help when you arrive, it is far better to move to another place where the surroundings are cleaner than to eat under such conditions. However, if the spot where you want to eat needs some cleaning up, do it. Because the previous picnickers left the place a mess is no reason you have to eat in its midst. Sweep the table and benches clean with your whisk broom. Wash off the table with a pail of water and wipe dry with old newspapers. Clean off the seats, if necessary. Lay clean newspapers on the table before spreading your tablecloth. Clean under the table and spray the area under the table with insect repellent. Do this before you lay your tablecloth.

Set your table as you would at home. Keep containers of food covered after serving from them so flies and other insects can't get at the food. Put a pot of water on the fire to heat for dishes after you have finished cooking your other foods so that you will have hot water for cleaning up.

When the meal is over have each member clear his place. If paper plates were used these can be thrown into the garbage cans with the leftover food still remaining on them. If plastic or aluminum plates were used, have each member of the family scrape his own plate into the garbage can or into a large paper bag placed on the ground at one end of the table. Have the picnickers wipe off their plates and silverware with paper napkins so the silverware and plates are ready for washing. Pick up any paper or food particles which have fallen on the ground and clean up the area around your table carefully so that it will be ready for the next family.

Now the dishwashing crew goes into action. The food committee sees to leftover foods. If you are staying for another meal, the food to be refrigerated is placed in the icebox. Cover the other foods and leave on the table in readiness. After the dishes are washed and dried they may be put at one end of the table and covered with a clean cloth until time to reset the table.

If you are having only one meal at the picnic grounds, the food and dishes should be cleaned up and the table cleared for the next occupants before the program of recreation begins. It is easier to clean up while everyone is fresh and full of steam. It is better to spend the first few minutes after a meal in activity that is not too strenuous. Cleaning up will give food a chance to digest. Stomachs are less apt to be upset if there is a waiting period before a session on the swings or slide or on the hiking trails or baseball diamonds. One upset stomach can ruin the day for everybody. Then, too, if the table is cleaned up, it is ready for the next family who may be waiting to have their lunch. It is not quite fair to hold a table all afternoon just for storage space if you have finished with it.

Planning the Menu

A picnic menu should be carefully planned. Foods that spoil quickly in the heat away from refrigeration should be avoided. A bout of ptomaine or food poisoning following a picnic is often the result of poor planning. Unless you have a way of keeping them refrigerated en route to the picnic and before mealtime, avoid salads with mayonnaise. Avoid chicken, turkey or fish salads with mayonnaise in them. Unless these are kept carefully refrigerated, these foods are ptomaine breeders. Avoid desserts such as éclairs or custard-filled cupcakes. Custard is a medium in which bacteria breed freely in warm weather. What is good for them is bad for you.

When taking cooked foods such as baked beans, scalloped potatoes, macaroni or rice casserole dishes, carry the foods in containers with tight-fitting covers. The leftovers can then be put directly into the refrigerator when you arrive at home, simplifying your clean-up problems at a time when there are many other details to attend to. If you come home with a pile of dirty dishes, with odds and ends of food to dispose of plus tired children to put to bed, the fun of the day is soon canceled out. Plan ahead so that homecoming is as pleasant as the going out. Don't let the delight of the day be ruined unnecessarily at the end.

In selecting the kinds of foods to take along, avoid too many hard-to-digest foods. Keep the menu simple and well balanced. Avoid rich and greasy foods. Since anything tastes good out of doors, select foods that behave better in stomachs that are going to swing on swings, slide down slides or go swimming. Simple foods are less trouble to prepare, are easier to carry and take care of and are less apt to spoil. They are just as filling and are far more healthful and are easily digested.

Suggested Simple Picnic Foods

Sandwiches—Make some at home. Cut into quarters and wrap only two quarters in each package. Less food will be wasted this way. Prepare only a few sandwiches at home and take the makings for more. The prepared ones will keep the children from starving to death. They can make their own if additional ones are needed at the picnic table. Lettuce will make the sandwiches taste even better. This can be added at the last minute at the picnic table.

Relishes—Celery sticks, carrot sticks, pickles, olives, cucumbers and tomatoes.

Fresh fruit—Grapes, apples, oranges, watermelon, plums, bananas, peaches.

Casseroles—Baked beans, potato salad made with vinegar dressing or mayonnaise (if you can keep it refrigerated), cole slaw.

Meats—Baked ham, sliced cold beef, cold cuts.

Beverages—Milk, coffee, iced tea, lemonade or orangeade.

Desserts—Cupcakes, cookies, tarts.

Cheese—A variety of sliced cheeses.

POTATO SALAD WITH VINEGAR DRESSING
(*Will keep safely unrefrigerated*)

Cook 5 potatoes in their jackets. Cool and peel. Cut up into small pieces or slice. Fry bits of bacon until crisp. Drain on paper towel. Make a vinegar dressing containing:

> ¼ cup vinegar
> ¼ cup sugar
> ¾ cup water
> salt and pepper to taste

Pour mixture into frying pan from which most of bacon fat has been removed. Add potatoes and heat through in mixture. Add bacon and mix through salad. If onion is desired, fry a finely chopped onion in a little bacon fat in the pan before adding the vinegar mixture, potatoes and bacon.

Picnic Cook-out

When a family wants hamburgers or hot dogs, the makings for these are taken instead of cold sandwiches. The hamburger should be mixed with seasoning at home and shaped into patties which are kept separated by pieces of wax paper or foil. These can be fried in a big frying pan or on a griddle. For those who want to cook their own, wrap a hamburger patty securely in aluminum foil and place above hot coals or a grill. Cook on each side for about ten minutes. Use long tongs to turn. A slice of onion can be placed in the foil with the meat and the two cooked together.

RECIPE FOR A GOOD FAMILY PICNIC

Ingredients

Take your own family of parents and children.

One carefully thought-out picnic plan (includes where picnic is to be, how long family will stay, when family will return).

One well-planned but simple picnic menu. (Not too great a variety and avoidance of rich and greasy foods which when combined with excited children often make for car sickness or middle-of-the-night upsets following the picnic. Avoidance of foods that spoil easily without refrigeration which may make for food poisoning.)

One operations plan assigning duties to each member of the family according to age and ability so that all the dirty work doesn't fall on Mother and Dad. These should include KP duties, helping with the preparation of the picnic lunch, packing up the picnic kit and the car, duties at the picnic grounds and general clean-up duties after returning home. Blend well so that everyone has some duties and picnic will end up a smooth affair.

One park within fifty miles radius. (Any greater distance and the children get restless in the car.)

One family picnic kit. (See description in this chapter.)

Directions for Blending

1. Get an early start. With all the family helping, this should not be too difficult.
2. When arriving at picnic grounds find a picnic table and clean up the surrounding area and the table thoroughly before unpacking the car. No sense eating in the midst of someone else's mess.
3. Unpack car. Everybody helps.
4. Give children free rein at this time to enjoy the facilities of the park. Give them a definite deadline when to return to table and agree upon a signal for recall when time approaches.
5. Father and mother set table and get food ready.
6. Call in wandering children using agreed signal.

7. No eating on the run. Everybody sits down and eats properly just as they would at home in the dining room.
8. Blend family and food leisurely and well. Do not hurry this part of the recipe.
9. When meal is completed, everyone helps to clean up. Wash all dishes. Don't carry dirty ones home. Repack the car.
10. One family-together activity is carried out. This can be a game of catch with bean bags, beach ball or baseball, a hike in the woods, a play session in the creek or any activity which takes full advantage of the natural facilities of the park area.
11. Mother and Father relax a while and give the children a free play period.
12. At the end of this period, children are called together. Family goes home early enough to avoid heavy traffic conditions on the road and before children are overtired. Leaving when everyone is still having a wonderful time and wishes he could stay longer is exactly the right time.
13. After arriving home, everyone carries out his particular duties and cleans up the after-picnic debris. A simple supper is served. Father and mother relax, children play until bedtime and the day comes to a comfortable close with everyone looking forward to the next picnic.

Note: You'll like this kind of picnic. It's not hard to make. It always turns out well and is popular with all the family. This recipe tends to make family picnic habit-forming and this is a good thing.

Variations: For variation invite other families to join with you. Uncles and aunts and grandparents can be sprinkled liberally throughout this mixture and will make the end result even better.

The Family Breakfast Picnic

Families should take advantage of the parks near their homes for a Sunday breakfast picnic. Get the picnic kit together the night before so you can get an early start. If you will not have time to get home after the picnic to change clothes before going to church, plan a simple cold breakfast which can be prepared without building a fire. Hot coffee or hot chocolate can be prepared at home and carried in Thermos bottles. If you do not have a car refrigerator, pack milk and orange juice in an ordinary pail with water and ice cubes. A tin can with a tightly fitting cover (such as a potato chip can) makes a good ice container as the water cannot spill or splash over the car interior. Cold cereal with fruits of the season such as berries, bananas or peaches, peanut butter sandwiches, beverage and fruit juices will prove an ample breakfast. Eating it out will make it a feast. Since no fire has to be built, no one need get too dirty. The leftovers will not be a problem. After breakfast the family can go happily off to church.

The Family Breakfast Cook-out

Morning is a wonderful time to be out in the park. There is a certain freshness about the air, the park is uncrowded and cleaner than it will be at the end of a picnicking day.

Get the picnic kit together the night before and pack into car as many of the props as possible so you can get an early start. The food that has to be kept under refrigeration, of course, is not packed until just before departure time. If this is a family project, then everyone in the family should have some responsibility for helping with the preparations. Assign definite duties to every member and spread the load of work.

If you have a picnic kit, include coffee pot and frying pan which are used just for this purpose. It won't matter if they get grimy and black with soot, so long as the insides of the utensils are clean. A coffee pot blackened from many fires only makes you look like experienced cook-outers.

Plan a substantial meal of bacon or sausages and flapjacks, or bacon, eggs and toast. The toast can be made directly over the hot coals. The bacon can be fried in the pan or grilled on toasting forks over the fire. If done on forks each child can be kept busy getting the bacon and toast ready while Father and Mother prepare the rest of the breakfast.

If several families meet together for breakfast it is even more fun.

The children can carry their breakfasts to the children's tables and the adults eat together at another.

The Church Family Picnic Breakfast

Churches have found that a standing breakfast date in a particular park makes for warm fellowship. Every Sunday during June, July and August, weather permitting, church families meet at an appointed place. Families bring their own food and cooking utensils. Coffee is made in a large pot community-style with the cost defrayed by the families sharing the beverage. The affair is timed so that after a leisurely breakfast, families go directly to church. Where a church has enough land around it to allow for a small picnicking area, the breakfasts could be held on the church grounds.

The Back Yard Cook-out Versus the Away-from-Home Picnic

Having a grill or fireplace in your back yard with a permanent picnic table or a folding one which can be carried out from the garage or basement makes outdoor meals a relatively simple undertaking. Certainly it eliminates traveling to parks. It makes summer entertaining easier since a large number of people can be accommodated without too much difficulty. It has its disadvantages, however. Eating out becomes commonplace instead of a treat. Mom still has the preparation to do but without the advantage of getting away from the house and enjoying a change of scenery. For Mom it means only a change of table but the same old kitchen. In other words, it means extra work for her without the accompanying rewards a picnic away from home affords.

If you are planning a back yard picnic and plan to entertain a number of families with children, remember that the accommodations of a yard are never so numerous or unusual as those a park offers. There will not be the playground or woodsy walks available which help to keep the children busy and entertained. A home picnic necessitates some arrangement for keeping the children occupied. The spirit of adventure and exploration is not so easily satisfied at a home picnic.

The flies and insects always seem more annoying at home. Somehow, the little discomforts we cope with at a picnic and accept as part of the game in a park or at the beach are just annoying nuisances at home.

It's fun to eat out at home, but an outdoor meal at home is not a picnic. For the most fun with picnics, widen your horizons and explore the unknown. The change is good for everybody.

12

Family Service Projects

There is an old French proverb which says, "He giveth nothing who does not give himself." Leisure hours given in volunteer service are manifestations of a strongly developed social conscience. Training in service begins at home. In an earlier chapter there was discussion relative to the importance of learning at an early age that there are some services performed out of love for people with no material gain in mind. Children can soon learn that there is great satisfaction in performing services for others.

In a home where the parents are active in service organizations, church or school committees, children gain a better understanding about the importance of giving service. If a parent is active in the P.T.A., for example, and through the efforts of this organization new playground equipment is installed in the child's schoolyard, he reaps the benefits of his parents' efforts. Parents in their home discussions about their volunteer services can point out what the results of their work can mean to their children and their playmates.

Schools, churches, Scout troops and other organizations working with children often give opportunity for their members to participate in service projects. The school has a paper sale to raise money for some new equipment. It collects money for the Community Chest and Red Cross and other worthy organizations. The children may be asked to bring books and toys to be sent to children in other countries as a good-will project. Churches send food and clothing parcels to children in distant countries and have the church school members help in this project. Scout troops raise money for their camp by selling cookies and candy. They sell brooms for the blind and help in the collection of funds in national drives for worthy purposes. Thus with home, school, church and community organizations all helping children to recognize their responsibilities as citizens to their communities and to persons less fortunate than themselves, the future volunteers in the world of service are being trained.

It is through service activities that individuals demonstrate their responsibilities as citizens toward each other and their communities. No community can afford through its private and public agencies to pay for all the necessary services which are so generously given by public-spirited citizens. The services of the paid employees are necessary, of course, but many valuable and important services are performed by trustees, volunteer corps, booster clubs, service organizations, Parent-Teacher Associations and others. There is no effective and worth-while organization which does not have behind it a large corps of volunteers who are, in truth, its lifeblood without which it could not long function.

Children who belong to Scout or Camp Fire organizations should understand that without the volunteers who act as leaders, these organizations could not long exist. The child who lives in a neighborhood which has no Scout troop because no leader can be found learns the hard way what happens if volunteers are not available.

Parents who sigh unhappily about the state of the world but turn down every request to act on committees or to give service in one way or another set poor examples for their children.

Service like charity should begin at home. If a child is brought up in a home where the mere mention of illness or trouble in a neighbor's home sets off a chain reaction of service activities, he learns by personal experience how important and satisfying it is to be neighborly. He may be asked by his parents to participate in this neighborliness by running an errand for or by mowing the lawn of the family in trouble. He will perform these services, his parents explain, with no expectation of remuneration other than the grateful thanks of the family involved. This is being neighborly, he is told, and no good neighbor accepts pay for acts of kindness.

As the child grows older he may participate in Civilian Defense programs as a ground observer or give service in hospitals where help is needed in getting patients to church service in the hospital chapel. He may become active in his school student council.

Through such experiences he learns to distinguish between acts of service and jobs for pay. While it is nice to be paid for some jobs, he soon learns that there are some services he performs for remuneration far more satisfying than money. The grateful thanks of a patient he has served or the warm expression of gratitude voiced by a neighbor or friend will come to mean more than anything money can buy. When a child learns this lesson, he has reached the level of maturity of which good citizens are made.

As he grows to adulthood, he may serve on the board of his church or service club. Through his service activities he may help to establish a children's camp, build a community center, launch a drive which results in better schools in his community or raise money for a valuable research project. The lessons in service he has learned at home bring benefits to his community and happiness to his own life.

"Service is the rent we pay for our room on earth," someone once said. The child who has been trained to use a portion of his leisure in service is one who will find his life good. Service activities give savor to our days and deep meaning to our years.

13

Tourists in Your Own Home Town

Have you ever visited friends in another city who took you on a tour of places of interest and at the end of the round confessed to you that they, too, were seeing some of these places for the first time? Have you ever on a vacation gone out of your way to visit a particular highly touted tourist attraction only to find it was not so attractive or interesting as something you have in your own home town?

One of the reasons vacations are such fun is that we take time out to do things and see places we never seem to find time for the rest of the year. Why ration holiday fun and limit it to two or three weeks per year? Take time out for a few hours per week to vacation in your own home town. The whole family can join in the fun. Make yourself an itinerary as carefully as if you were planning a European tour and follow it as faithfully.

You've never pretended you were a stranger in your own home town and explored it as you would a city in which you are passing through on vacation? Then you've a treat in store for you. Adventure lies ahead. Pleasant surprises will be your fate. You'll discover it's like finding money in the pocket of an old suit you haven't worn for a long time.

There is an old saying: "When in Rome do as the Romans do." We simply rephrase it and suggest: "When at home, do as you would if you were in Rome!"

PLAN YOUR TOURS

Gather the family together. Explain that you are going on a series of sight-seeing trips. Every member of the family old enough to make suggestions gets into the act and names places he'd like to see. Those old enough to do research are given duties to perform. One may be delegated to dig out information about historic places of interest in his home city. Another may search for information about buildings of particular interest. Confine your trips to a radius of fifty miles at first. Later you can begin the process all over again extending the range to a hundred miles. In picnicking season pack a lunch and enjoy it in a roadside or state park en route. In winter plan to eat in some exciting restaurant along the way.

Resources for information in your town might be:

1. The AAA—The Auto Club, if you are a member will furnish booklets and information about near-by places of interest. A trip-planning expert will be able to give helpful and valuable information. He will have city maps showing the city and county parks and other spots of interest.

2. Chamber of Commerce—Visit the Chamber offices and pretend to be a newcomer. You'll learn fascinating facts about your town. They can tell you about industries which welcome visitors. They may suggest a tour of the river edge or lake front. Perhaps there is a Coast Guard station you can visit. Ask if there is a round-house where you might be permitted to watch activities. Find out if there is a vantage point where you can watch the molten wastes of the steel mill being poured out onto the slag heaps. Try to ascertain when the mills will be pouring. The possibilities, you will find, are almost unlimited. The chances for adventure, excitement, unforgettable experiences are yours within easy reach.

3. Newspaper Offices—Your city newspapers will have travel editors, industrial, garden and sports editors. They will be wells of information about places to visit and things to do in your own town.

COMMUNITY RESOURCES TO VISIT

1. Museums—You may have a nationally known museum in your town which has featured programs and exhibits. You've probably put off visiting it because you know you can go any time. Write

or call the various museums in your city. (See the classified pages in your telephone book.) Ask for their printed circulars which give the hours they are open and the program of events to come. You will be amazed at the wealth of information and opportunities for fun and education available to you. How many of the museums in your town have you never visited? How long has it been since your last visit? Put the museums on your itinerary and schedule a visit to each one. You may have in your city or near-by community:

     a. Museum of Art
     b. Health Museum
     c. Museum of Natural History
     d. Historical Museum
     e. Science Museum

2. Industrial Exhibits—Some industries have permanent collections of products and exhibits relative to their industries. You may have such an opportunity in your town. Examples of these are: Auto and Aviation Museum Exhibit of the Thompson Products Company in Cleveland, Ohio; The Corning Glass Works Mu-

seum in Corning, New York; Atomic Museum in Oak Ridge, Tennessee; The Science Museum in Chicago, Illinois.

3. Zoo—No matter how often you visit a zoo, there is always something of particular interest or some animal antic to tickle your funny bone. Take a child with you whenever possible. You see the world with recaptured joy and wonderment through a child's eyes.

4. Botanical Gardens—Botanical gardens are always beautiful, but at certain seasons they are breath-taking in their beauty. Visit special exhibits but also at other times when the smaller crowds will allow you to view the various plants at your leisure.

5. Aquarium—If there is an aquarium near you, count on spending some time there. Every member of the family will find it fascinating.

6. City Greenhouse—Perhaps the Parks Department of your city maintains a greenhouse where plants are raised for park gardens and flower beds, where trees are kept in nurseries before they are set out on the streets and where exotic and tropical plants are raised. Occasionally the greenhouse will have a special event such as an African violet show, or a special display of certain species of blossoming plants. A greenhouse is another spot to visit several seasons of the year as the show is ever delightful and always changing.

SPECIAL SIDESHOW TRIPS

1. Visit an apiary and observe the bees at work in their honey factories. See how the honey is processed before it comes to your table.

2. Don't miss visiting a maple sugar bush if you are in a part of the country where this is possible. Watch the newspapers so you know when the sap is running and the sugaring-off begins. Once you've been to a bush and seen all the labor that goes into making a can of maple syrup you'll have a new appreciation of your breakfast treat the next time you pour it over your pan-

cakes. Don't miss the maple syrup festival. See the sugar being made. Perhaps they will let you beat some of the heavy syrup into candy yourself.

3. Find out when your farmer friends will be threshing and request permission to come and watch. Observe all the safety precautions and stay out of danger's way. You'll find they do some things differently since Grandpa was a boy.

4. Visit a pear, peach or apple orchard in picking time. Stop at a cider mill during apple season and taste the cider as it comes out of the presses.

5. Stop at an old grist mill where the grain is being ground as it was years ago by the old millstones powered by a water-driven millwheel.

6. Visit a dairy farm and let your children see where the white stuff usually seen in bottles and cartons really comes from. Watch the cows being milked by hand or machine.

7. Visit a farm that has diversified crops. Show the children the chicken house, the hog pens, the cow barns, the granaries and haymow. If you are lucky enough to visit when there is a new calf or a litter of pigs your enjoyment will double. When you've gone home, write the farmer and thank him for the privileges you've enjoyed. The children can add their little bits to the letter telling what interested them most.

8. Perhaps there is a sports arena in or near your home town. Take in a ball game with the family. Watch a soccer match some afternoon. See a hockey or football game.

9. Stock car racing will give the family a thrill. On the way out have a picnic lunch at a roadside or state park or stop at a special restaurant for a treat for the whole family.

10. Visit a track where harness or horse races are held. Visit all the places at the track that you normally see only in the newsreels. See the winners' circle, stand along the fence to watch a race, watch the horses being exercised. Absorb all the atmosphere but let the other fellows make the bets.

11. Tent or barn theaters are fun in the summer. Take the family to

a stock company production when the play is one the whole family can enjoy.

12. Historical Spots—Visit historical monuments or tombs. Stop at an old cemetery and take time to read some of the old headstones. Try to reconstruct a family history from some of the statistical data on the stones in family plots. Visit sites of old battlegrounds or replicas of old settlements. Take time to discuss some of the historical facts which are represented there.

13. Special Events—Watch the newspapers and billboards for announcements of special exhibits or shows which may be coming to your city. Visit a sportsmen's show, flower and garden show, food show, do-it-yourself or hobby show. Watch for special attractions held in department store auditoriums.

14. Special Exhibits—Watch for and visit special exhibits which will be of interest to the family members. Stamp and coin exhibits, defense exhibits, etc. are often free and worth your time.

15. Fairs—The county or state fair is an important part of everyone's education. The exhibits, the midway, the horse races and special features will keep the family interested for hours. Take your lunch and plan to spend the day.

16. Special Tours—Visit a dairy in your city. Observe how the milk you drink is processed. You'll be amazed how much care is exercised by the dairy and your city health department to safeguard your family's health.

17. Visit a newspaper particularly at a time when the presses are running. Since many large papers conduct tours for groups, you may be able to join a group going through.

18. Visit a greenhouse just preceding a holiday when flowers are particularly beautiful. Just before Christmas or Easter are both good times. Visit a greenhouse that specializes in vegetables.

19. Visit the water purification and sewage disposal plants in your city. It gets a bit lonely in those places on a Sunday afternoon and the men on duty are more than glad to show you around and explain the processes employed. Check in advance to be sure you will be admitted. You may need a special pass.

20. If you were on a tour of Europe you'd more than likely visit historic churches and cathedrals. If yours is a cosmopolitan community as most American cities are, there will be churches of all denominations, of all types of architecture with particular points of interest. Attend some of the special services. Christmas or Easter mass in a Greek Orthodox Church is a rare experience to an outsider. Since the Greek Orthodox calendar is different, check with the church for correct dates and hours.

21. High Spots—Visit the observation tower or a spot with a view. Take your field glasses and camera with you. Try to identify familiar spots.

22. Visit an airport. Watch the planes coming and departing. Observe all the different kinds of services that must be taken care of before the plane takes off again. Field glasses will add to the fun.

23. Tour your city or home area during Christmastime to view the lights and decorations. Finish off the evening with a stop at a drive-in for a special treat.

24. Spots of Natural Beauty—At springtime, tour the country looking at the flowering trees and shrubs. Take a walk in the woods and look for the first spring flowers. Look for the signs of the earth coming back to summer life again. The miracle of the strength of the new shoots which must push their way through the obstacles of hard ground, dead leaves, stony paths is ever new and ever wonderful.

25. In summer drive through the country and see the colors of ripening wheat and the flowers of fields and meadows. Try to identify the various crops you see growing. Play a game as you go along naming the various products that come from the crops. Can you identify the crop that gives you your flour or your roasting ears, the buckwheat for your pancake flour or the plant from which soybean products are made?

26. In fall, make a tour of the areas where the fall coloring is especially beautiful. Stop at a roadside stand and buy the apples crisp and fresh from the trees. Enjoy some of the fresh cider. Buy your

jack-o'-lantern pumpkins for Hallowe'en and bright-colored gourds. Get popping corn that you have to dry and shuck from the ears yourself.

27. In winter just after a heavy snow, drive to one of your favorite parks. Walk over the familiar trails now disguised and camouflaged. Watch for the tracks of the wild animals. Walk over the new snow and be the first to leave a footprint. When you get back to the car enjoy a cup of something hot you've brought in a Thermos bottle. Hot tomato soup or tomato juice or a hot chocolate tastes like ambrosia after a winter hike.

28. If yours is a city with large concentrations of nationality groups visit some of these special areas. Perhaps you'll see a bocci game being played in "Little Italy." If you have a Chinatown, plan to have a meal there and let the Chinese waiter recommend some special Chinese foods to you. Try eating some of your meal with chopsticks. Your waiter will be pleased to show you how.

29. On a summer day, be a tourist in your own home town and take a trip in the special sight-seeing bus. There will be times you'll wonder if you are really in your own city or far away in some strange place.

30. Make a point of seeing a parade at least once a year. They are always exciting and interesting.

31. If you always go everywhere by auto, try using public transportation in your city sometime. Ride a particular bus or train from one end of the line to another. Pick a line that will take you through parts of the city you rarely travel.

32. If your children have never been on a train, take a short train trip some Sunday making the return trip the same day. Be tourists in the city or town where you will have to stop over for the return train.

33. If yours is a city with ocean, lake or river transportation, drive along the waterfront. Park awhile and watch the activity along the docks and piers. Try to identify the various kinds of ships and boats. Visit a lighthouse. Take a short boat trip.

34. Cultural Programs—Attend an orchestra concert or a choral pro-

gram. Dance concerts by nationality groups or modern dance or ballet companies are enjoyable and interesting to all members of the family.

35. Natural Phenomena—Caves, waterfalls, hot springs and interesting rock formations are always fascinating to visit. Visit them at different times of the year when they will look completely different from the last time you saw them.

36. Let your family join an organized bird walk. Take your field glasses as well as your bird books. With an expert to help you identify the birds you see, you'll learn more quickly and have fun while you learn.

Take pictures of the places you visit. Include family members in the pictures you take. If the pictures are prints, make a scrapbook of your tours. If you have slides or movies, show them in a series as you would your vacation pictures. They will be interesting for years to come. You and your friends will be amazed at how much you've seen. You'll find you've learned a lot of facts and had fun doing it. You will have created many happy family memories that will come to life again every time you look at the pictures.

14

Family Traditions

Every family should have its traditions. These are the bright threads that run through the fabric of everyday family living, enriching lives and brightening memories. It does not matter whether the traditional customs are centered around some religious observance, are based upon a nationality folk custom carried here from another continent or are just some particular little tradition which came about accidentally when something happened which the family enjoyed and vowed to make it into a custom to be observed regularly at a particular time. These observances add joyousness to family life. More, in these days when the pressures are to conform and to be like everyone else, traditions add diversity to everyday living and make for a richer culture. Traditions are the customs which give a family its individual characteristics. They are the things that set my family apart from yours, not unkindly in any derogatory way or in any way which belittles your family because it is different, rather it makes mine more interesting to you and yours of interest to me.

These little differences when carried on as family traditions and customs contribute to feelings of unity and strength. Because they are enjoyable, traditions tend to strengthen family feeling in each individual member. Members entertain a healthy feeling of pride in family.

In the United States of America, made up as we are of peoples of many racial, religious and national origins whose traditions enrich our culture, it is important that we encourage and nurture differences. Diversity is the lifeblood of a democracy. It tends to stimulate growth whereas conformity and similarity stifle and smother it. In the dictator-ruled countries, conformity is the rule and diversity a crime.

WHERE DO FAMILY TRADITIONS BEGIN?

Religious Traditions

How and where does a family tradition begin? Many are religious in origin. Every religion has its holy days with their traditional patterns. In Judaism, more than in the Christian religion, the religious traditions are closely related to family life. Many of the traditional observances are held in the home with the entire family joining together. In the Christian religion, the special holy days are commemorated or celebrated in the church and not in the home. There is unfortunately no equivalent in Christianity to the Seder, the feast which commemorates the exodus of the Jews from Egypt which is celebrated in Jewish homes on the eve of the Passover or by the orthodox Jews on the eve of the second day. Jews also have a traditional ceremony in the home on each Sabbath eve. The mother begins the ceremony by blessing the candles both in Hebrew and English. She prays after lighting the candles: "Blessed are Thou, O Lord our God, King of the Universe, who has sanctified us by the commandments and commanded us to kindle the Sabbath lights." The father often calls the children to him and blesses each individually. At Yom Kippur, too, the father blesses the children. In some homes, this blessing ritual may also be observed at the beginning of the new calendar year as well.

Christmas and Easter, the two most widely celebrated of the Christian holy days which have become occasions for families to come together, differ in context from the Seder celebration in the Jewish home. The religious aspects of these holy days are celebrated in the churches. Around these Christian holy days customs related more to folklore than to religion have sprung up. In the churches at Christmas, the services recall the Christmas story with the Christ Child, the Wise Men, the stable at Bethlehem, the shepherds and angel choirs and the biblical prophecies. The celebration at home most often centers around Santa Claus, the Christmas tree, gifts and Rudolph the Red-Nosed Reindeer. Similarly after the solemn observances on Good Friday (at church) and the joyous celebration of Easter Sunday commemorating Christ's victory over death, the home celebration seems to bear no relation to the original concept. The Easter bunny, Easter baskets, colored eggs and other gifts and the traditional ham dinner are the order of the day.

The point we would like to make here is that if the Christian family would have certain religious traditions as part of the family life, they must create their own whereas in the Jewish family these are part of their religion and the celebration in the home is a long-established pattern. Some Christian families traditionally say grace at meals and may have a family worship service on Sunday evening. In some homes, the blessing of the children by the father on New Year's Day is an established family tradition. The important factor is, however, that the teachings of the church whatever its denomination be carried over into the life of the individual, into family and community life. The church may do its part well but the good is lost if the teachings are not carried beyond the church doors and applied to situations which arise in everyday living. The establishment of family traditions with religious bases could do much to relate religious teachings to everyday situations and could do much to establish better behavior patterns.

We are concerned here with the togetherness, the feeling of family unity which is fostered in family celebrations more than with the reasons for the observances or the manner in which they are celebrated. Whether the religious observances are solemn or joyous in nature does not detract from their value in building and maintaining family unity. Memories of joy centered around family living need not always be uproarious and hilarious. Joy can have its solemn moments when feelings run so deep that tears of joy may well up. These moments, too, are memorable and serve as sources of strength to carry us through periods of deep sadness and misfortune.

Traditions of National Origins

Perhaps yours is a family with deep pride in its national origin. Proud to be Americans they are, but proud, too, of their origin and eager to carry on those national customs which enrich their lives and make their family life interestingly different. One family will celebrate Christmas Eve with a smörgasbord with traditional Swedish dishes. Mother and Aunt Selvig and Grandmother will slave for days in the kitchen preparing one hearty dish after another. Meat and fish dishes of many types, cheeses and all the delicacies that mean the old homeland fill the board. The younger generation will wonder why they go to so much trouble, when a steak dinner would be less effort and taste just as good. Righteous indignation follows such an outrageous proposal. Not now but years later will the younger members look back and remember those family gatherings and sigh for the "good old days." Old family recipes will be looked up and brought back to life, not only because the food tastes better and different but because it is flavored with happy family memories.

In your family there may have been a custom that grew out of a single occurrence that turned out to be so much fun the family decided to continue it from year to year. Perhaps at Christmas one year, each child found a particular kind of stuffed animal in her stocking. Somehow that animal was *the* present of the year. The following Christmas, Mom and Dad remembering the popularity of that gift placed another such animal in the stocking. The cherished little animals become part of a collection and may be set up on a particular shelf labeled with signs which say "Miss Christmas of 1953," "Mr. Christmas of 1954." And somehow for that family, it wouldn't quite be Christmas without stockings stuffed with the special Christmas animals.

Another household may enjoy some little family joke on a particular day. On Ground-Hog Day, the traditional food may be ground hog. And what does it matter if it looks and tastes like pork sausage to the casual visitor? It's ground hog to the initiated and no one will ever convince the members of that family to the contrary.

The passing down of a family tradition gives a wonderful feeling of continuity to family life. It is a little touch of immortality. Mother carried on the same tradition that was practiced in her home when she was a little child. Now we pass it on to still another generation. Perhaps the original reason for the tradition or custom is long since lost, but somehow it is fun to do it because it belongs to our family and no one can take it away from us. We may let it die, but no one can kill it but ourselves. This is ours. This is a part of our family that to us is as important and distinctive as our family name.

The feeling of pride that prompts us to say, "Now that isn't the way the Joneses do it—not this Jones family anyway. This is the way we do it," may very well strengthen and give us courage to stand up for a particular principle when being different may be somewhat painful and when we stand alone or with a small minority. It may well be that the traditions which help us to preserve diversity of action and belief may give us courage to stand up and be counted for what we believe no matter how alone we stand. A parent faced by the age-old argument of youth who asks, "Why can't I do that? All the other kids are doing it?" can give answer: "In our family we do some things differently. We try to use good sense even if it means being different. And what you want to do is not good sense no matter how many others are doing it." And in a family where members have learned to treasure the traditions that make it different, the parent may be able to help the child to see the reasonableness of such an argument and abide by its decision for his own good.

Whether you agree that family traditions may have other useful by-products or not, if you agree that they can be fun and every family ought to have a few, some suggestions follow which may help you in strengthening those you already have or help you in building some new ones or reviving some forgotten ones.

RELIGIOUS CUSTOMS AND TRADITIONS

Grace at Meals

When we attend a community-wide meeting or church supper, the meal is usually preceded by the saying of grace. And for this brief moment, the noise which is always a part of such an occasion is stilled, and where there was confusion and diversity of thought and conversation, there is a moment of quiet when minds and thoughts are united for a few words of prayerful thanks. In a world where many are hungry and where the peace and freedom we take for granted are nonexistent for millions, it seems only good manners to take a moment and recount our blessings and to say "Thank you."

For many families the saying of grace is a loved custom. As one person puts it: "We always said grace at home. Now we are all grown and have homes of our own. We're scattered all over the country. Most of my brothers and sisters have carried this custom into their own homes. Somehow, when I stop to say grace at mealtimes, it seems my whole family is reunited for a moment. For wherever they are, when they sit down to eat, they say grace too. We may not actually be eating at the same time, but that doesn't matter particularly. We all know that at that moment when we stop to say thanks we are together again for a moment, if only in thought. It's comforting somehow. It tells us that if the need arises to stand together, we can do it. It is good to know and to remind yourself that you have a family behind you. It is the most terrifying feeling in the world to feel that you are alone."

Some simple graces are given here. They may be said by one of the various members of the family taking their turn or by the family in unison.

Simple Prayers for Grace at Meals

Father, giver of all good, accept our praise and bless this food. Amen.

Father, bless this food and make us ever thankful. Amen.

Our Heavenly Father, bless this food to our use and us to Thy service. In Jesus' name we ask it. Amen.

Lord, we thank Thee for the blessings of this day. We thank Thee for this food, for friends and for fellowship. Amen.

Father, bless this food and keep us ever mindful of our responsibilities toward each other. Amen.

Our Father, for food, for friends and for all good things make us truly grateful. Amen.

Our Father, for this food and for all the gifts of life, we thank thee. Amen.

15

Family Fun on Vacation

A pseudo-family vacation is one in which Father announces that since he is the breadwinner and this is his vacation (and he has a point there) he is entitled to go on the kind of vacation he wants and everyone else must fall in line, because that is the way it is going to be. Once he has made his declaration, the plans proceed from there. After due process, the family is packed and ready.

Father is anxious to get to his fishing camp up north. The family gets off to a middle-of-the-night start. Six or seven hundred miles later, with as few stops along the way as possible, with everyone so tired and cranky a lighted match would set off an explosion in the car, they arrive at camp, cross and hungry, tired beyond words and faced with all the unpacking to do, the beds to make, supper to prepare.

Stumbling back and forth from camp to car (because of course it is dark by this time) to the accompaniment of the cries and quarrels of the overtired children, Father, stiff and sore from a too many hour drive, beset by all manner of irritating things that inevitably happen on a long trip when getting there in a hurry is the only consideration, finds his vacation getting off to a jolly start.

The first day, Father takes Susie and Junior fishing. In an hour or two they have their fill of just sitting in a boat. Father has to row them back to the dock just as the fish are beginning to bite. After that Father fishes alone. The interminable days follow. Father spends long hours in the boat fishing—just what he loves to do. Mama tries to keep the kids amused, fights mosquitoes and flies, cooks on an old wood stove and tries to time her cooking so that when Father comes in with the day's catch, everything will be ready to eat by the time Father cleans and cooks the fish as only Father knows how.

After ten days of fish for lunch and dinner (that's the way Father likes it and "if you are hungry you'll eat") and a few days of rain when the flies and mosquitoes are especially hungry, everybody but Father is counting the days to going-home time.

Finally the vacation draws to a long-time-in-coming end. Father fishes until the last minute. Everybody gets to bed early the night before departure. Cheerfully everyone gets up at two in the morning to pack up and get off to a three-o'clock start in anticipation of another long and jolly drive home. Each mile seems like two. Drivers on the road are unusually stupid. Father wonders how they ever got their drivers' licenses. A suggestion for a stop along the way had better be backed by sound necessity. Father wants as little delay as possible in the headlong rush home.

Home at last, the dreary job of unpacking is accomplished in jig time. Everyone falls gratefully into his own familiar bed. Father has loved his vacation so much he has, of course, waited until the last minute to get home. He cheerfully contemplates the prospects of getting back into the harness the next morning, turns on his back and snores his way through the night. Mother breathes deeply, happy to be home, and looks forward to several wonderful hours in the laundry where in the morning the electric washer full of hot water and detergent will transform piles upon piles of dirty garments into clean, sweet-smelling wearing apparel again. She even has time to plan the next evening's menu which she will prepare in her own bright kitchen on her good old electric range before sleep drugs her and she sinks into oblivion. Junior and Susie are already asleep, too tired to dream, lulled by the happy realization that Father's vacation is over for another year. Thus we draw the curtain on the pseudo-family vacation according to Father.

Father does not know it yet but, next year, he will have exactly the same kind of vacation with one difference. He'll go *alone* or in the company of other fathers who love that kind of vacation. Mama and the kids will go off to visit Grandma and everybody will have a lovely time!

The real family vacation is one planned by the whole family with the comfort and wishes of everyone given fair and careful consideration. The planning together adds the fun of anticipation to the plan and helps to eliminate some of the unpleasant situations which arise from lack of careful preparation.

PLANNING THE VACATION

First Planning Stage—Where Shall We Go?

Will it be to a beach, the mountains, the country or just a keep-on-the-move and see-all-we-can vacation? Take a vote of the family members and try to arrive at a conclusion that pleases everybody. Mother will need some relief from her usual cooking and housekeeping duties, the kids may not enjoy what the adults want, but try to reach the happy medium which will please some of the people some of the time. There has to be some give and take when a number of people of different ages are involved.

Second Planning Stage—Mode of Travel

If you are going by plane, bus, train or boat make reservations early. Try to plan your travel time early in the week when schedules are less crowded. Weekday travel rates are often cheaper than weekend rates. Save money and trouble by planning accordingly. Don't schedule your return trip to get you home at the last minute. If you hit a delay somewhere you won't arrive home in time. The worrying and tension resulting from delays can undo all the good of your vacation. Plan carefully and then relax.

If you are going by family car, limit the distance you plan to travel. Two weeks do not give you time to go to the moon and back. Don't plan to drive more than three hundred miles in any one day. Even that doesn't allow too much time for sight-seeing and rest stops. Long days of riding are boring to children. One discontented and unhappy child can infect everyone else in the car. A carful of unhappy people is not conducive to vacation fun. Limit your distances and increase your chances of fun.

Third Planning Stage—Plans Along the Way

Get good, up-to-date road maps. A detour can be unpleasant at any time, but when it comes at the end of a long day's drive in strange country just as it is getting dark it can be exhausting. If detours are indicated on your route, plan to be through them while it is still early in the day.

Once you know your route, mark the places of interest you want to visit and allow enough time to enjoy them fully. Plan rest stops regularly. As you drive along let the members of the family take turns deciding on a stop. One member may select a certain time. For example, Susie may say: "Let's plan to stop for a cold drink at two o'clock." The refreshment stand that comes into view about that time gets the family business. Junior may select a historical signpost as the next stop. The car stops, and the family reads the text on the signpost before travel is resumed. The subject of the signpost may give the family a topic of conversation for the next ten miles with everyone racking his brain for facts remembered from history lessons and textbooks. The next stop may be Dad's. He may say that at four o'clock he has a surprise in mind for everybody. Since he has studied the road map carefully, he may know that about that time they will be near a state or national park area where he plans to stop and take time out for a hike along the trails through the woods. Mom's surprise may be something to be enjoyed en route. At a certain hour she may distribute a special treat of candy or fruit which she has hidden away. Maybe she has purchased pinwheels, balloons or some other toy which she distributes. Each surprise is fun for the entire family. If each member has to figure out at least one treat a day for the other members, all are kept busy planning and anticipating the fun everyone will have when the surprise is sprung. If there is fun en route, the vacation is fun all of the time and the trip coming and going is something to enjoy rather than something to endure.

Stop early in the day to find lodgings. Your choice of places will be greater. Try to find a place near a swimming pool, drive-in theater, picnic spot or place of historic interest. Each stopover then becomes a fun spot during the on-the-way or coming-home part of the vacation and will be as much remembered as the fun at the vacation spot itself.

Remember, too, that getting back is part of the vacation. If you have a long ride back home much of the good you will have derived from your vacation can be canceled out in those last few days. In any event, try to get home a day or two early so you can have time to relax at home before starting back to work.

Fourth Stage—Where to Stay

Will you be visiting friends or relative at your destination, staying in a resort where meals will be served or will you be in a cottage or cabin where you will do most of your own cooking? In the latter two situations you will need to make reservations well in advance. If you plan to stay in a cottage or cabin you will have to know what necessities are furnished and what you will need to take with you. You will want to know what recreational facilities are available so that you will have the right kinds of equipment with you. If you are doing your own cooking, how close will the nearest store be? You may want to do some advance grocery shopping at home to be sure you can get the varieties of goods you want or any special foods certain members of the family need.

Fifth Stage—Taking Precautions

Someone in the family allergic to certain pollens? Stay away from areas where these flourish. No one has a good time if one member of the family is in misery during the vacation period. Check with the Pollen Survey Committee of the American Academy of Allergy, Fourteenth and Sheridan streets, North Chicago, Illinois, for information about areas which are relatively pollen-free.

Stay away from areas where communicable diseases have been reported in epidemic stages. There is nothing worse than having one of the children come down with measles in the middle of your vacation and miles from home. Check on polio possibilities before going to a particular area, particularly if you are traveling during the epidemic season.

Check on the safety of water supplies in areas where this might be questionable and plan accordingly. Always carry a container in the car holding safe drinking water.

Fortify yourselves with medicine which prevents car or motion sickness. A pill in time saves upsets.

Carry a well-equipped and complete first-aid and medicine kit. There may not be a corner drugstore handy when you want to administer medicine for a minor disorder or upset. A good kit includes these items plainly marked:

FOR FIRST AID	FOR MINOR UPSETS
Burn remedy	Aspirin
Sterile gauze	Laxatives
Adhesive tape	Enema bag
Band-aids	Medicine for motion sickness
Scissors	Salt tablets
A mild antiseptic soap	
Sunburn preparations	

Poison ivy remedy
Baking soda
Brown laundry soap
Bug bite remedy
Antiseptic
Needle and tweezers for slivers
Ammonia

If any member of the family requires special medicine, have a good supply on hand and an extra prescription which can be filled along the way if necessary.

For the member of the family who can't see without glasses carry an extra pair or an extra prescription, just in case.

If one member of the family has a heart condition or has just recovered from a serious illness, better have the doctor tell you just how much that individual can stand and what he should and shouldn't do.

Traveling with Baby

If you plan to take the baby be assured that he can travel as comfortably as anyone. Dress the baby comfortably. Take as many disposable or washable clothes as possible. Carry a plastic bag for washed things that didn't dry in time to travel. Keep the baby comfortable in a basket or folding car bed. Take the familiar doll or toy and a gadget for heating the bottle through your car cigarette lighter or in a convenient electric socket. Take the baby's regular toilet seat along too. A small car icebox will keep a day's supply of the baby's formula fresh.

If the baby is on evaporated milk, preparing the formula is simple. Sterilize the bottles the night before and fill to the required level with boiled water. Just before feeding time, wash a small can of evaporated milk, puncture the can and add the necessary amount of milk to the boiled water.

Carry the baby's favorite canned foods with you or purchase a few days' supply along the way. Carry the child's favorite dish and feeding spoon. Don't forget an opener which will open jars, cans and bottles.

The Vacation Itself—Live to Enjoy It

The kids are usually fit for almost any kind of activity. It's Dad who has to be careful not to overdo physically. Eight hours a day behind a desk is not good training for hours of strenuous physical activity for two weeks of the year. The least unpleasant thing that can happen is a set of screaming, aching muscles. One lives through this type of discomfort but a vacation is more fun without it. A broken bone or a heart attack is infinitely worse. Let discretion be the better part of the vacation. Follow all the health rules and you'll live to enjoy your vacation.

Eat normally. "This is vacation and to heck with the calories" may be the philosophy which spoils your vacation. An overindulgence in rich foods, alcoholic beverages or too many sweets to which you are unaccustomed will do more than increase your waistline. You can upset your entire digestive system and have a miserable time.

Don't try to get that healthy-looking sun tan in one day. This temptation is hard to resist as manufacturers of sunburn remedies will testify. None of us would deliberately put his body into a hot furnace and give himself a first- or second-degree burn. We would call anyone who did that all kinds of a fool and question his sanity. Yet every summer millions of people foolishly allow the sun to burn them to the blister stage. During the pain-filled hours following such a burn they practically take the pledge. "Never again," they swear. Then as the pain subsides and the blisters dry up and begin to peel, they brag to their friends and fellow workers about the terrible sunburn they got on vacation. Their friends smile sympathetically and proudly show their own scars. Next summer experienced but no wiser they go out and do it all over again!

You'll pay it no heed, but here is a sun-tanning formula which will get you tanned without a painful burn:

Adults: Fifteen minutes the first day. Increase the time gradually day by day.

Children: Babies under two years of age five minutes limit.

Fair-skinned anybodies: Face up to it. You aren't the sun-tan type. Better be fair than blistered!

Caution: Beware those cloudy days when the sun can burn you unexpectedly. Be careful where you get reflected rays as well as direct rays when you are on the beach or out on the water in a boat. Watch the time and take cover.

Heat exhaustion and sunstroke are no fun. Consult a physician immediately. Better still avoid courting such disasters and eliminate the necessity for a cure.

Safety First—Stay Alive on Your Vacation

If we thought about all the dangers that we are exposed to each day we'd never get out of bed. If we considered all the possibilities for accident which face us during vacation, we'd never leave home. Nevertheless, consideration of these dangers and simple precautions are often the best preventives of disasters which may do more than ruin a vacation.

Danger lurks in many places. Trouble lies in wait for the uninitiated and unprepared. We have mentioned the danger of overexertion after periods of sedentary living. A danger list follows. Don't be ashamed to be cautious. Safety rules have been made from experiences —sad, disastrous experiences. Don't let anyone "con" you into believing that caution and cowardice are synonymous. When you gamble with safety you gamble with your life and the lives of your loved ones. LIVE by the rules. You may DIE without them.

SWIMMING SAFETY

Never swim alone. No matter how good a swimmer you are *never swim alone.*

Swim only in safe unpolluted water.

Know your swimming place before you do any diving. Check for hidden rocks, sudden change of depths, undertow, etc.

Don't go in the water too soon after eating. Wait at least an hour after eating and longer after a heavy meal.

Let your body get accustomed to the water gradually. Don't shock your system by plunging into cold water without preparation.

Remember when you swim far out you still have to swim back Don't overestimate your prowess and strength.

BOATING SAFETY

Know your craft and the idiosyncrasies of its type. Don't try to behave in a canoe as you would in a flat-bottomed rowboat.

Don't overload any craft.

Be sure all nonswimmers or poor swimmers are equipped with lifejackets before going out. Protect the children especially. They move so quickly they are out of the boat before you know it.

Be weather-wise when you go boating. Some bodies of water are especially dangerous in sudden storms.

If you are a landlubber don't risk your life and those of your family by trying to be a one-day admiral. Take a boat ride with an experienced boatman and enjoy the ride. You'll get all the thrills without any of the spills.

FISHING SAFETY

Fishhooks often hook more than fish. Don't cast over another's head. Before you cast look back at your lure and follow it with your eyes until it hits the water.

Don't jerk a snagged line to free it. Row over or walk over to it and get it loose. A jerked line may snap back toward you.

Don't swing a sinkered line when anyone is within range. A sinker when flying free from a broken line is a dangerous missile.

DRIVING SAFETY

Drive as if every other driver on the road were a blind beginner without a brain in his head.

Observe all speed laws.

Observe all safe driving rules.

Don't drive when you are sleepy. Stop and nap or take a refreshment break.

If you wait until five minutes after you should have been there to start back home, every driver on the road will be against you. Get an early start, give yourself plenty of time and you'll see how the other fellow's driving has improved since the last time you were in a hurry.

Don't be afraid to give the other driver *your* right of way. It's better to be alive than dead right!

Be sure your car is in good condition before starting out on a long trip. A car in good mechanical condition, properly serviced and with good tires will probably get you there in good shape and in good time.

Change drivers frequently. A change every fifty miles before a driver even feels tired makes driving easy for everyone.

FOOD SAFETY FIRST

Safe water and pasteurized milk are things you want to be sure of. Don't take it for granted that all milk served in public places is pasteurized. Accept only a properly labeled carton or bottle. If it is not, use condensed or dry milk and mix your own. Boil questionable water for ten minutes to be sure it's pure. Don't use questionable water to wash your dishes or clean your teeth unless you boil it first.

When eating in public places avoid creamed foods, mayonnaise-type salads, custard- or cream-filled pastries, and cold chicken or turkey salads. You can't be sure they are safely fresh or well refrigerated. Don't court food poisoning. It's bad enough to have when you are home, but while you are on vacation it's infinitely worse. If you suspect food poisoning get to a physician as quickly as possible.

Don't eat a lot of seafood if you aren't used to it unless you are sure you don't get an allergic reaction from it. Don't do too much experimenting with unusual and unfamiliar foods when you are away from home.

Indulge yourself but not to extremes. There are other ways to be kind to yourself that will bring you more pleasure than overindulgence.

When visiting in strange country, don't eat strange berries, fruits or mushrooms no matter how much they tempt you until you know they are safely edible.

WEATHER SAFETY

Listen to the local weather report as you vacation and act accordingly. If you are traveling in a bad storm or predicted hurricane area, take cover and weather it out comfortably and safely. Don't take your chances on the road. Get to a motel or tourist area. Use the time to play cards, read in bed or get in a little extra sack time.

If you are caught out in an electrical storm get to shelter if you can do so quickly. Your car is the safest shelter. Take shelter in a cave or under a cliff. Don't stay under an isolated tree or take cover in a shed or barn which is out in the open. Stay away from wire fences, high points or wide-open spaces. If you are caught in wide-open space, lie down. Don't be the highest object in that area; you make a too-convenient lightning rod. The best precaution is prevention. Don't let yourself get stranded far from shelter in bad weather. Storms usually give some warning. Don't start out if one is threatening. Start back to shelter at the first sign of bad weather.

POISON IVY SAFETY

It is wise to be acquainted with poison ivy, poison oak or poison sumac, but don't get too friendly. All parts of the plants are toxic. People who are very susceptible to their poison may be affected not only by direct contact but by touching something that has been in contact with the plants. Clothes, tools, animals which have touched the plants and even smoke from burning plants may be infectious to some people. A brief description of each plant and a sketch follows. The best cure is careful avoidance of any such plant. But if you aren't sure, wash yourself thoroughly with laundry soap when you come in from a walk in the woods. Clean any clothes you think may be contaminated.

POISON IVY

Poison ivy grows as a woody vine, a shrub or a trailing climbing vine. It is closely related to poison sumac and poison oak. Three rounded oval leaflets about three inches long on one stem are your

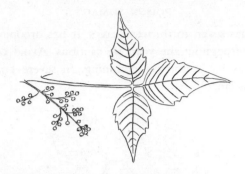

first warning. Not all vines with three leaves are poison ivy, but if you are not sure the vine is not poison ivy give it a wide berth and be safe. Poison ivy has small greenish-white flowers which become a white berry-like fruit similar to that on mistletoe. These berries may cling through the winter. At all stages all parts of the plant are poisonous.

POISON OAK

In Western and Southern United States, poison oak plants have wavy leaves shaped much like oak leaves though they are not related

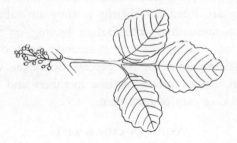

to the oak. These leaves grow in threes. They are usually glossy but sometimes may be fuzzy. All parts are poisonous. The leaves of poison oak and poison ivy are green in summer, red in fall and are usually shiny. The oil which makes all the trouble is the substance which makes the leaves shiny.

POISON SUMAC

This plant has seven to thirteen leaves. It has drooping clusters of white berries throughout the year. Be cautious. Avoid contact. Treat infected parts as for poison ivy poisoning. In severe poisoning cases consult a physician.

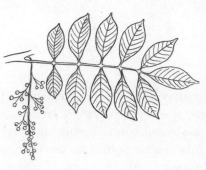

HAPPY VACATION HINTS

Peace-of-Mind Department

There are certain precautions to take before leaving on a vacation to allow you to go with a carefree mind. Some have been mentioned before but they are listed here briefly as they are sufficiently important to mention more than once. Before leaving on vacation make several check lists placing each on a separate piece of paper. Some lists must be taken care of by the parents. Some can be checked off by the children. Assign lists to various members and hold them responsible for taking care of each item.

THE CAR CHECK LIST

1. Car checked for mechanical defects?——
2. Brakes okay?—— Tires?—— Lights?—— Spare?—— Battery?—— Cooling system?—— Windshield wipers?—— Door and trunk locks?——
3. Road maps up to date?——

4. Trouble kit in car?—— Flares?—— Flashlight?—— Jack and tools?—— Car first-aid kit?——
5. Car comfort equipment?—— Pillows?—— Blanket?—— Motion sickness pills?——

THE HOUSE CHECK LIST

1. Arrangements for boarding out the pets?——
2. Notify police you'll be away?——
3. Cut-off service?—— Newspaper?—— Milk?——
4. Forwarding address at post office?——
5. Arrangement with neighbors to look in occasionally?——
6. Last-minute checks. Lock all windows and doors?—— Leave light on in a couple of rooms?—— Disconnect all electrical appliances?—— Turn off all gas burners?—— Turn off gas heater?—— Leave all pilot lights burning?——

FAMILY CHECK LIST

1. Dental checkups for each member?——
2. Medical checkups for each member?——
3. Special medicines in good supply for trip?——

FUN KIT CHECK LIST

Vacation is filled with hours to get in pleasures that everyone is too busy for other times of the year. Take a family fun kit which includes some of the items on the following list. Take time as a family to play a game of cards or some other favorite game. Take craft projects along to fill an occasional hour making useful projects. Take time to read the books you never get time for otherwise. Save these special activities for the rainy day or for that last couple of hours before bedtime in your cabin or motel. Plan a quiet hour each day (other than nap or rest time) to enjoy quiet activities. Put all equipment into a shopping bag with handles and carry it in with the luggage.

1. Games such as Parchesi, Chinese Checkers, Monopoly, etc.
2. Decks of cards for card games, solitaire

3. Knitting, crocheting, leather projects, Indian beadwork, weaving, etc.
4. *Popular Mechanics* and similar magazines. Take the past few issues from home that you haven't had time to see.
5. Books from your book clubs you haven't had time to read, paperback mysteries and novels
6. Modeling clay that doesn't harden
7. Crayons and coloring books
8. Puzzles and peg boards
9. Chalk, slate and eraser
10. Scissors and cutouts

Vacation Explorer's Kit

There will be new views, open skies, new fields to explore on your vacation. Be prepared to see and learn as much as you can about the new country you are traveling through. Include in your explorer's kit some of the following:

1. Guidebooks to nature about birds, wild flowers, the stars, trees, insects, reptiles, marine life, shells, rocks, etc. Be prepared for all of the new things you will see. Inexpensive guidebooks are available at your bookstores.
2. A couple of good hand lenses. Inexpensive three-power lenses can be bought in your local five-and-ten-cent store.
3. A pair of good binoculars. You'll have fun with these when you want to identify a bird, a plane, a ship or the license plate on the car ahead of you. Carry them with you when you visit observation towers and other high points.
4. Use your cameras to record some of the interesting sights you see. Sometimes you need concrete evidence to convince your friends and neighbors you aren't telling tall stories.

Snack Kit

Keep a snack kit well supplied with emergency foods for those times between meals when everyone is starving to death. The kit will come in handy in the motel just before bedtime or along the highway when a rest stop is desired and a roadside table comes into view. Include such snack-makers as:

1. Individual packages of cookies, crackers, pretzels, potato chips
2. Jar of peanut butter, glass of jelly, plastic knife for spreading
3. Chewing gum, wrapped hard candies, suckers
4. Cans of tomato juice, orange or other fruit juices. Keep paper cups in this kit along with a can opener.
5. Small cans of canned fruits such as mixed fruits, pineapple, applesauce, pears. A can of fruit eaten with some peanut butter and crackers is a satisfying snack. Keep plastic spoons handy. It's fun to eat out of the can hobo-style.

Roadside Camper's Kit

Eating out picnic-style helps save money and adds to vacation fun. Roadside tables, roadside parks and public picnic areas are readily available in most states. Well-balanced meals can be served quite easily with a minimum amount of equipment. A list of equipment and hints for picnicking the simple way follows.

1. Portable cook stove (one two-burner gasoline or canned gas stove)
2. Plastic dishes and stainless steel flatwear
3. Gallon Thermos jug. Keep this filled with fresh cold water so you always have water to drink, for making fruit-ade drinks and for washing dishes and hands.
4. Aluminum foil for broiling hamburgers, roasting ears of corn, baking potatoes, etc.
5. Paper napkins and paper plates for short stops when you don't want to take time to wash dishes
6. Set of plastic cereal bowls. These are fine for soups, fruit cups, cold cereals, hot canned vegetables, ice cream.
7. Extra Thermos to carry hot water taken from your last overnight stop. Hot coffee or tea is quickly made when you start with hot water. Hot water added to canned soups gets lunch ready faster. Use hot water for dishes and for clean-up purposes.
8. Paper towels do for dishes as well as hands. Keep detergent in a plastic bag so it doesn't spill out of the box into all your other

supplies. Use soap-treated steel wool pads for cleaning pans and flatwear. Use a sponge for washing dishes and cleaning up.

9. Carry a plastic tablecloth to cover the picnic table with. Old clean newspapers always come in handy for cleaning off tables and as a protection for your plastic cloth.

10. A small portable charcoal stove is handy to have but not necessary.

11. A car icebox will keep milk fresh, butter (in jar) sweet, vegetables, eggs, bacon, fruit in good condition.

12. Dishes can be washed in cooking pots or a hand basin which will fit into a picnic kit without too much trouble.

13. Coffee pot

14. Sauce pans with tightly fitting covers

15. One large frying pan (cast iron) with cover

16. One large cooking pot with tightly fitting cover, preferably aluminum. Also doubles as a dishpan. Several mixing and serving spoons.

17. One pancake turner

18. One sharp long-handled fork

19. Large and small carving knife which can be given a good sharp edge for cutting meat, vegetables and bread

20. Two good paring knives

21. Knife sharpener

Shop Along the Way

Rest stops can be shopping stops at roadside fruit and vegetable stands and supermarkets. If you keep a small but good stock of canned goods, dry cereals, milk, fresh fruit, eggs, butter and bread, you can have well-balanced meals much cheaper than you can eat out with all the fun of picnicking thrown in for free. Replenish stocks often and keep inventory low.

CANNED GOODS AND STAPLES

Canned mixed fruits, pineapple, grapefruit
Canned juices, orange, citrus mix, grape juice, pineapple

Canned soups
Relishes, sweet pickles, dill pickles, pickled beets
Condiments, salt, pepper, mustard, chili sauce, catsup
Dry cereals
Canned prepared foods, baked beans, corned beef or roast beef hash
Salad dressing, French or mayonnaise
Canned meats, wieners, dried beef
Tea, coffee, instant chocolate milk mix

FRESH FRUITS AND VEGETABLES

Lettuce, carrots, corn (when you can get it fresh), tomatoes, cucumbers
Apples, oranges, bananas, melons, pears, peaches

OTHER FOODS

Bacon, eggs, cheeses, peanut butter, jellies

SUGGESTED ROADSIDE MENUS

BREAKFASTS

1. Fresh fruit (melon, orange, banana, peach)
   Bowl of dry cereal with milk
   Scrambled egg with toast or sweet roll
   Coffee, tea or milk
2. Fruit juice (orange, grapefruit, grape, pineapple or mixture)
   Bacon and egg
   Toast (toasted over fire)
   Coffee, tea or milk
3. Dish of berries, sliced peaches or sliced orange
   French toast with butter, syrup or jelly
   Bacon fried in pan or broiled over fire
   Coffee, tea or milk
4. Dry cereal with fresh fruit (berries, peaches or banana)
   Toast with butter and jelly
   Coffee, tea or milk

LUNCHES

1. Bowl of hot soup
   Peanut butter and jelly, cream cheese and jelly or cold meat
   sandwich
   Fresh fruit and cookies
   Coffee, tea, lemonade or milk
2. Fruit cup made with canned pineapple or grapefruit as base
   with sliced fresh fruits added
   Hot wiener sandwich
   Carrots sticks, pickled beets, pickles, sliced tomatoes
   Cookies
   Fruit-ade, coffee, tea or chocolate milk
3. Hamburger patty
   Hot or cold canned baked beans
   Lettuce, cucumber and tomato salad with or without dressing
   Relishes, pickles or pickled beets
   Fruit and cookies
   Coffee, tea, milk
4. Tomato juice, hot or cold, or hot tomato soup
   Toasted cheese sandwich (Put butter in frying pan. Put in cheese
   sandwich. Fry until bottom slice is brown. Turn over and
   brown top slice.)
   Lettuce and tomato salad
   Ice cream and cookies
   Coffee, tea, milk
5. Fresh fruit cup
   Western sandwich (Fry loose ground meat in pan, with or
   without onions. Pour off excess fat. Pour beaten eggs over meat
   mixture and cook until egg is firm. Serve in toasted hamburger
   buns.)
   Sliced tomatoes and carrot sticks
   Cup cake or cookies
   Coffee, tea, chocolate milk
6. Bowl of hot chicken soup
   Crisp bacon and peanut butter sandwich
   Melon, peaches, pears or berries and cookies
   Coffee, tea, milk
7. Fruit juice drink
   Heavenly hot dog sandwich (Broil hot dog over fire or fry in
   pan. Put in wiener bun with stick of cheese. Wrap whole
   contraption in foil and put over coals long enough for cheese

to melt. Remove and add your favorite condiment or pickle.)
Tossed salad made with lettuce, cucumber, tomato, carrots
Bananas sliced and mixed with canned pineapple
Coffee, tea, milk

8. Bowl of hearty vegetable soup, Scotch broth or some other
filling thick soup
Scrambled egg in sandwich bun
Fresh fruit and cookies
Coffee, tea or milk

SUGGESTED DINNER MENUS

1. Broiled hamburgers
Cooked fresh or frozen vegetables
Potatoes wrapped in foil and baked in the coals
Sliced tomatoes
Fresh fruit and cookies
Beverage
2. Broiled pork or lamb chops (Be sure they are broiled slowly
and are well done.)
Cooked minute rice
Cooked fresh or canned vegetable
Cucumber, lettuce and tomato salad
Cake or cupcakes
Beverage
3. Spanish rice made with minute rice, ground meat, canned
tomatoes, green peppers and onions
Head lettuce salad
Fruit and cookies
Beverage
4. Chili made fresh with ground meat, onions, kidney beans and
canned tomatoes, served with crackers
Lettuce, pineapple and cottage cheese salad
Gelatin dessert (purchased ready-made and kept in icebox until
eaten)
Beverage
5. Broiled sirloin steak
Fresh roasting ears (Clean, wrap in wet paper towels and foil
and roast over the coals on the rack.)
Tomato and lettuce salad
Melon
Beverage

6. Broiled chicken (Cut in pieces and broil slowly about 40 minutes
   on the rack over the coals.)
   Potatoes wrapped in foil and baked in the hot coals
   Sliced tomatoes and cucumbers
   Fresh fruit and cookies
   Beverage
7. Fresh-caught fish (which you have purchased or caught and
   cleaned yourself) can be broiled over the coals on a rack.
   Dip in or brush with melted butter, oleo or bacon drippings,
   season and broil.
   Baked sweet potatoes wrapped in foil and baked in the coals
   Mixed fresh vegetable salad
   Melon
   Beverage
8. Fresh fish dipped in egg and flour and fried in bacon drippings
   Baked corn on the cob
   Pickled beets
   Fresh fruit and cookies
   Beverage
9. Tomato juice
   Fried corned beef or roast beef hash
   Hot canned wax beans or any favorite vegetable
   Lettuce, tomato, cucumber salad
   Fruit cup and cookies
   Coffee, tea, milk

OTHER SANDWICH SUGGESTIONS

Cheeseburgers (Fry hamburgers in pan, put in bun, add slice of
cheese, wrap in foil and put over fire until cheese melts.)

Bacon and egg sandwiches (Cut bacon in small pieces and fry until
crisp. Pour off most of grease. Pour in beaten eggs and scramble
with bacon bits. Serve in a bun.)

Bacon and tomato sandwiches (Fry half slices of bacon until crisp
and drain on paper towels. Toast bread over coals. Put sliced
bacon, sliced tomatoes, lettuce and mayonnaise on toast.)

NOTE: Save dessert until later in the afternoon and stop for an ice
cream treat along the way.

Prepared gelatin salads and desserts or cottage cheese can be purchased in supermarkets and kept cold in your car icebox.

Dinner Roadside Park Style

Usually you serve dinner after you have stopped for the day and are safely settled in your cabin or motel for the night. You can relax over the evening meal knowing that you have a bed for the night. You look forward to time in the picnic area and willingly stretch out the dinner hour. Try to get finished before it gets too dark to see what you are doing when you clean up.

If you've had luck finding fresh-picked corn and good meats in a clean well-stocked market, you can make dinner a wonderful treat. While lunches must be rather hurried affairs cooked over the portable stove, dinner is the time you get out the charcoal grill or use the grills supplied by the park.

Tricks of Cooking over Charcoal

Start your fire with paper and kindling and then add charcoal. Allow fire to burn to red coals before attempting to broil any meat.

Keep a pan of water or a squeeze spray jar such as is used to sprinkle the clothes handy near the fire. When dripping grease causes the flames to spring up, spray or sprinkle the flames with water. This will kill the flame but will not extinguish the fire in the coals. Meat broiled over coals kept under control in this fashion will not be charred. The meat or chicken will cook slowly and thoroughly without becoming blackened.

Keep seasonings handy and season the meat or chicken as it cooks.

When baking potatoes in the coals, if they are wrapped in foil they will not become blackened. Put in coals about forty minutes before you expect to eat them. Chicken takes the longest to do, hamburgers the shortest so time your potatoes to be done when the meat is done.

Corn wrapped in foil and baked on the rack needs to be turned frequently, but takes about ten minutes at the most to cook satisfactorily.

Special Vacation Adventures

Each vacation should have its special adventure. During the winter while vacation plans are still in the incubator stage families should keep a weather eye open for ideas and suggestions for adventure on the vacation. Suggestions may pop up in magazine articles, books on travel and adventure or newspaper articles. The idea suggested may be the one that determines the place and type of vacation which the family will eventually settle upon. For example one of the children may read an article on the ruby mines in the Franklin, North Carolina, area where tourists are permitted to mine all day for a small fee. The chance of finding a valuable ruby may be slight but the fact remains that some persons have found them. No one ever believes it will be the other person. Such is the optimism of man. The idea when introduced to the family may so intrigue them that immediately plans for a tour of that general region begin. The urge to mine rubies may take the family to that beautiful Smoky Mountain region where they can hike in the mountains, visit the Atomic Museum at Oak Ridge, Tennessee, see Norris Dam, live for a while on the Cherokee Indian Reservation, attend an outdoor historical pageant and have a wonderful time in general. The whole plan may come out of the one suggestion to mine rubies which may turn out to be the high spot of the trip whether any family member strikes it rich or not.

Certainly hunting treasures always has appeal. Treasures may be seashells to be gathered freely on sea and lake shores, turtles to capture and take home for pets, semiprecious stones to be found on shores, on hillsides, in abandoned mining areas, driftwood and other treasures to be combed from beaches, butterflies for collections or photographs of historical or scenic spots. It is good to have such a treasure-hunting expedition in mind when a vacation is planned. It is a rare individual who is not stimulated by the possibility of discovering treasure in unexpected or expected places. The authentic antique picked up for a song, the specimen of rare or valuable rock formation, the bag of shells or pine cones which will afford hours of fun at home in the hobby room during the winter months often bring more pleasure than any other part of the vacation. This is the portion of the vacation that lasts and brings pleasure for months and years to come. These treasures are the conversation pieces which stimulate good talk when friends come to visit or when the family gathers together years later. These are the things which recall happy hours of years past and make vacations live forever.

Vacations for Parents Alone Are Important in Family Living

However much there is to be said about the importance of families vacationing together, there remains the fact that it is equally important for Father and Mother to have a vacation alone without the kids. Family togetherness is not always best fostered by keeping the family together on all occasions on all vacations. Sometimes a two- or three-week separation of parents from children does more to nurture family unity and closeness than a similar period together. The parents need time to be away from their children when their own interests can be satisfied without concern as to whether the children will enjoy such an experience or not. The parents need a chance to be husband and wife and discard the roles of father and mother for brief periods when they can be concerned about each other without interruptions by the children. The second, third and fourth honeymoons are as important as the first in maintaining a good marriage.

Father and mother will do well to plan an occasional excursion, however short, away from their children if the children can be satisfactorily farmed out to grandparents, aunts and uncles or friends who are happy to keep them. If they consider it a privilege and joy to have the children come and not a chore to be performed in martyr-like fashion to give the parents a chance to be alone together, it will be a happy occasion for everyone. If the children know they are welcome and wanted, the period away from their parents will be a happy one. If the parents are satisfied the children are in good hands where they will be cared for and loved, their minds are free to enjoy their brief respite from the responsibilities of parenthood.

Similarly it is good for children to spend a vacation at an organized camp. There are many valuable lessons to be learned and there is much to be gained from a good camp experience. At the end of a successful camp session, home looks mighty good to the children. The parents have had a chance to enjoy a period of freedom from the responsibilities of the children and are glad to see them return.

The period of homesickness, if successfully weathered, is good training for the necessary future separation when children grow to adulthood. Parents, too, need the training in enjoying their lives without the children so that they can face the eventuality of giving up their children and allowing them to attain maturity and live their own lives when the time comes.

There is a time when Father should have his vacation away from his family, when he can go off on a fishing or hunting expedition with just the boys and rough it to his heart's content. In later years he will probably want to include his son.

There will be times when the man of the family will attend business conventions alone or with his wife, the latter occasion giving the parents a chance to have a few days away from home to do things alone and together. These can serve as valuable respites from family cares which parents need occasionally.

Mother, too, needs the chance to be away for a period with "the girls" renewing acquaintances, meeting old friends again at college or sorority reunions. She needs the chance to participate in Parent-Teacher conventions, League of Women Voters meetings or other conferences or conventions where opportunities to satisfy certain lifelong interests and the chance to be away from home cares are happily combined.

So, while there is a time for togetherness in family life there must be a time for being apart. Each is necessary to the healthy development for each member of the family. Each is necessary for the good family life. Each sustains it and nourishes it.

16

The Fun of Working Together

The old-fashioned roof-raising, corn-husking, threshing parties or quilting bees were happy social affairs in pioneer times, but much hard work accompanied the gaiety. The early pioneers understood and applied the principle that working together for a common goal could be fun. The joys of companionship are not necessarily limited to play activities and when applied to a work project they are augmented by the satisfaction which comes when a job is well done.

This principle can be effectively and successfully applied to family life and can contribute to family solidarity. When a father and son have worked side by side at a particular job and the son has supplied the correct tool at the right time or carried his share of the load or applied his strength to a task that could not have been accomplished without it, more than the job has been accomplished at the end of the day. The two can look at the finished job and solemnly shake hands in mutual pride over their accomplishment. Dirty and tired though they may be, they can say and mean every word: "It was a tough job, but wasn't it fun?"

Certainly father and son relations were strengthened that day. New understanding of each has had a chance to develop. Each has had the opportunity to see and appreciate the talents, strength and abilities of the other. There is a warmth of companionship, too, that comes from a shared experience. It is from occasions such as these that a boy will be prompted to boast to his friends: "My Pop is the strongest, smartest guy in the whole world, I bet. You should see him handle a saw. Paul Bunyan had nothing on him!" Father is probably bragging

to his associates, "You should see that kid of mine work. He kept right up with me all day. He worked as hard as any man. And catch on fast! Man, he can run that tractor as well as I can!"

The son has learned more than how to do something new. He has come to know that work can be fun and there is a good feeling inside when you have done your share and done it well. Years later, both father and son may look back on these hours as some of their happiest memories of family life.

Similarly, mother and daughter may share the duties of preparing the meals, doing the laundry and cleaning the house. Work hours are shortened because of the extra pair of hands and the time passes pleasantly when there is company on the job. A good relationship develops more readily between mother and daughter. Talk comes more easily when hands are busy. Confidences are exchanged more readily and naturally than they would be if a parent and child made a deliberate effort to "sit down and talk things over." In addition, the daughter is learning homemaking skills and arts which will be valuable to her when she establishes her own home. Because she will know and understand some of the responsibilities that face her as a wife, mother and homemaker, she will be better prepared for marriage. For a girl to enter marriage bragging that she doesn't know how "to boil water" is nothing less than tragic. There is nothing appealing about the helpless woman who has been permitted to grow up in a home entirely ignorant about the work necessary to running a household successfully. The mother who has done everything for her daughter and never asked her to lift a finger in her own behalf or perform any household task has hardly done her child a service. The daughter will not always be in a protected situation where mother or servant will do all her work for her. She may find herself on a camping trip as one girl did, and assigned to KP duties which in this instance meant washing the dishes. The girl stated haughtily: "I don't know *how* to wash dishes. *My* mother has a dishwasher!" Another girl who was to assist in the clean-up duties said proudly: "*My* mother has a dishwasher too. *Me!*" One needs no second guess as to which statement was given better reception by the other girls on duty.

Many children are being raised on the principle that work is work and fun is fun and never the twain join hands. Work can be fun. Without work there can be no fun. Each is as much a part of living as night and day. Sometimes a particular duty can be an annoyance when it conflicts with a fun activity, but never to have work, that part of living that gives dignity and meaning and purpose to life, is the most tragic circumstance of all. No one understands this better than the worker who has retired from a busy work life to doing nothing. For a brief period, doing nothing is novel, but prolonged inactivity can become an unbearable burden.

Children need chores and work activities to give meaning to their lives. This is an important part of training for the work life of adulthood. These tasks should not be just busy-work but must be purposeful activities that contribute to and are necessary to family well-being. Even the youngest child can be assigned a duty which has importance. Emptying the wastebasket or garbage container is a very simple but important duty. The value of the latter to the family welfare is pungently understood if the job of emptying it has been thoughtlessly neglected. Washing dishes is another simple but necessary task. A sink piled high with dirty dishes may be a laughable situation in a cartoon or comic strip but to the homemaker it is no joke.

Some of the tragic problems of today's youth center around the fact that they do not have enough work activities to perform on a regular basis. In a rural community a farm boy or girl will have definite chores which are related to the family livelihood. The needs of the animals cannot be ignored or sloughed off easily. The chickens and hogs and cattle must be fed. Cows must be milked. Weeding, hoeing and cultivating of the crops must be kept up. There are few excuses strong enough to be acceptable for failing to do one's duties where the livestock or the crops are concerned. The city boy, however, unless his parents assign definite chores and duties has nothing as necessary or purposeful to do. He may, when he is old enough, take on a newspaper route to earn spending money. But more important than the money he earns is the discipline of the job. Newspapers must be delivered regularly regardless of weather, beckoning ball fields or other temptations which may provoke him to desert his duties.

Youth with its boundless energy cannot tolerate idle hands. If there are not enough useful and important jobs to be performed and steady discipline to enforce the performance of the assigned duties, the idle hands will be put to tasks not always socially acceptable. What may start out as mischievous behavior motivated by boredom may later end in delinquent acts.

Training for life with its understanding of the purpose and necessity of work and its place in everyday living, the understanding of duties and responsibilities toward duty can be taught and learned at a very early age. Such understanding must be developed in the home and is the responsibility of the parents toward their children.

The parents can list the jobs of the home which can be performed by the children. Some will be on a daily basis, some on a weekly, some on a less frequent basis. Some duties such as spring housecleaning, cleaning the basement or attic will be only occasional. Duties should be assigned to each child according to age and ability and added to or made more difficult as the child matures. Some parents prefer to pay for the jobs. Others do not pay wages but give the child a regular weekly allowance for spending money. Some good arguments for paying for the jobs are:

1. A job done for pay must be performed according to the standards of the person doing the hiring. Therefore a boy who washes windows for his mother must do them to her satisfaction just as on any job he must satisfy his boss before he is paid for it.

2. A child learns more about the value of money if he is paid by the job. For example, a child may want a particular toy or novelty which takes his fancy. The cost of the desired object translated into so many piles of dishes or so many lawns to be mowed may help the child to make the decision whether or not it is worth the price. If he wants it badly enough to spend his hard-earned money on it, he must really want it. If the child later finds he has made a foolish purchase, the lesson learned is a good one and is learned at the expense of his own pocketbook and not his parents'!

3. When a job is paid for, it must be done when the employer wants it done and not when the employee finds it convenient. This eliminates much argument about jobs around the house. If a child knows that the lawn must be cut by no later than Saturday noon and he wants to play baseball on Saturday morning, then he must arrange to do it sometime Friday if he expects to satisfy his employer. A child thus learns that work responsibilities must take precedence over play activities and play is a reward to be enjoyed the more because it has been earned.

4. Since girls cannot always find outside jobs as readily as boys, pay by the job in her own home gives a daughter a chance to earn her spending money.

Some parents, on the other hand, prefer to give a child an allowance and impress upon the child that each member of the family has certain family duties and responsibilities that represent his contribution to family life. Children should learn that there are many tasks about the homes that may be unpleasant and even distasteful to the parents which they nevertheless must perform day after day. The parents do these jobs and find them tolerable out of the love they have for their children and for each other. Children should be helped to recognize that they, too, have an important role in the maintenance of family well-being. They need to learn that there are certain duties which family members perform out of love and devotion and recognition of responsibilities, not just for pay. It is never too soon for children to learn that love and devotion must be given freely. They cannot be bought; they must be earned. Doing for each other is one method of earning love; it is one method of paying in kind. With such understanding love of a child for parent, parent for child, sibling for sibling, love of the individual for humanity in general is developed on a sound basis. With this kind of love, life becomes more than existence. Life, then, has real meaning.

Children trained in a home that develops such an understanding will appreciate the service professions of teaching, medicine, welfare work in which the worker gives unstintingly of self, often far beyond the call of duty without too much concern about the reward and often at a salary which would be laughed at by a factory worker. Children thus trained will appreciate more the teacher whose devotion to her job leads her to teach the individual as well as the subject; the doctor who gives devoted service to his patients; the nurse who performs the most unpleasant tasks with grace, tenderness and cheerfulness; and the youth leader who gives hours and hours of time to help young people find their way in a confusing world.

Children trained to recognize their responsibilities early in life will grow to mature adults who are cognizant of their duties to their communities. And whether they enter the service professions or work as volunteers in their churches, schools and communities, they will be doing the jobs that need to be done to make life better for their children, their neighbors' children and the children in many generations to come.

SUGGESTED LIST OF HOME DUTIES
FOR CHILDREN OF ALL AGES

Since the jobs assigned are necessary to family well-being as well as being practice for living, it is important that the children develop good work habits while they work. Parents who are concerned about giving their children good training will insist that these duties are performed not only faithfully and well but without complaint. The list follows:

1. Wiping the dishes when mother washes
2. Washing the dishes while brother or sister wipes
3. Washing and wiping the dishes
4. Emptying the wastebaskets
5. Keeping the garbage container clean
6. Burning the waste papers
7. Sweeping the kitchen
8. Keeping one's room neat
9. Making one's own bed
10. Mowing the lawn
11. Shoveling snow
12. Picking up one's toys when play period is over
13. Stacking and bundling newspapers and magazines (The child may then sell them and keep the money.)
14. Running errands
15. Washing windows
16. Vacuuming the rugs and dusting the furniture
17. Scrubbing the kitchen and bathroom floors
18. Taking care of pets (feeding, bathing, cleaning cages, etc.)
19. Washing the family car
20. Weeding and cultivating the garden
21. Raking leaves
22. Helping with the spring and fall housecleaning
23. Painting or wall washing at spring and fall housecleaning periods
24. Helping with the preparation of foods (peeling potatoes, washing the salad vegetables, scraping carrots)
25. Setting the table (When a child is too young to handle dishes, he or she may set the silverware and napkins in place.)

26. Bringing in the milk from the milk box or back door
27. Hanging out the wet laundry (A young child may have a special line hung at a low level and be given the task of hanging the socks and handkerchiefs only.)
28. Helping with the week-end shopping
29. Helping with the family ironing (A young child may begin by ironing handkerchiefs, hand towels, washcloths and dish towels and take on more complicated items later.)
30. Carrying the rubbish and garbage containers to the curb on collection days and returning the empty containers to their proper places
31. Sweeping the garage floor and keeping the garage straightened up
32. Helping with the cupboard cleaning job (It is very helpful to have someone to hand things to when some of the cupboards are high ones.)
33. Keeping the linen closet neat
34. Shining one's own and Daddy's shoes (A well-equipped shoe-shining kit makes this fun.)
35. Helping with the mending (sewing on buttons, learning to darn socks)
36. Bathing a younger sister or brother
37. Baby sitting with younger brother or sister
38. Feeding the baby

WAYS TO MAKE WORK FUN

There are many ways to teach children that work can be fun. Some suggestions follow. And since this is a fun book, some games to play while working at some tasks are given here too.

Pride in Quality

Work becomes satisfying and fun to do if a sense of pride in quality can be developed in the young worker. High standards must be required of the child on his job. Sincere praise follows when standards are met. Gradually the child adopts the standards imposed as his own. He will find pleasure in a job well done whether or not there is someone to praise him at the completion of the job. His own satisfaction is reward enough. When pleasant memories, too, are associated with the task, any job can become a pleasant relaxing occupation. For example, sock darning (almost a lost art these days) is usually a tedious, unglamourous task, but to four little girls it was a pleasant summer afternoon's entertainment.

In the author's family there was a favorite Aunt Louise. In visits to her home two nieces and the two girl cousins darned socks together. Each had her own small jelly glass as a darning ball and her sock project. Aunt Louise took singular pride in her neat smooth darns. In teaching her daughters and nieces, she was able to impart her own high standards to the four little girls. To have an open space in the center of a woven square or a rough spot which would rub and blister a heel was unthinkable. Rivalry developed among the girls, each trying eagerly to win Aunt Louise's approval and to outdarn the others. Memories of this little class in homemaking art are pleasant ones. There was as much talk as there was sewing in this cozy circle. Any tediousness of the job was lost in the fun of the moment. The girls, now grown women, often think back to these happy hours as they mend socks now. The standards of this day are kept high in Aunt Louise's memory.

A child can be trained to find satisfaction in a job done well and make the job a challenge instead of something to be endured. Pride in a shiny cooking pan, a row of scoured shining knives, the shining white cleanliness of a sink polished with fervor, the orderliness of a freshly raked yard or recently weeded flower bed are rewards enough to anyone who has been trained to take pride in a job he does well. Many a monotonous, backbreaking job becomes an interesting challenge.

A child trained in this manner will appreciate and blossom under praise but will mature to the point where his own satisfaction in his job will suffice. He will know when he has done a good job and will not need anyone to tell him so. He will know, too, that no amount of false flattery will make a good job of a poor one. The test for maturity comes when the good standards trained into him become his own. He will soon learn that doing a particular job in a sloppy way will not only result in an unsatisfactory conclusion, but will make the job hard to do because the challenge of quality is lacking.

Pride in Speed

As a child develops a skill in a particular task, praise at the speed in which he has accomplished the job (providing quality is maintained) will also be a motivating factor in making work fun. A child who does a good job of washing and drying the dinner dishes but putters around three hours doing the job needs to be encouraged to speed up the process. The parent might set a particular time deadline. Setting the timer or an alarm clock on the stove might serve as a challenge. It is understood that the job must still meet standards, however. The time allowed in the first speed test should be sufficiently long for the job to be accomplished well. The next time, it might be cut down five minutes, the third time another five minutes until a reasonable working minimum is reached.

To make the challenge even more fun, a surprise reward is offered if the time goal is achieved. The rewards are small bits at first. When the final goal is reached, the reward is appropriately larger. At first it may be an unexpected candy bar or the promise of a play period with Mom and Dad. Of course, once the goal is reached, that continues to be the expected time limit for the job. No reward is then offered or expected. The shorter work time is its own reward as it leaves time for pursuit of recreational interests and activities.

Pride in Acquiring Skills

A child often expresses an interest to do some household task because he wants to do what the father or mother is doing. The novelty may soon wear off. The wise parent who wants the child to learn particular skills which will be helpful to him for all his life must employ methods to keep the child interested in that task so that his skills improve with time.

Dad allows the child to work with him in the home workshop. The child may have his own set of tools. While Dad repairs the garage door, the child is learning how to take a wooden crate apart, carefully prying the boards loose, pulling out the nails without splitting the boards, etc. While Dad saws a large plank, Junior cuts a piece of orange crate with his own small saw. He hammers when Dad hammers. There will come a time when he can work side by side with his father and uphold his end of the job with skill. He may even make suggestions which will make the job simpler or better than the way Dad had it figured.

Mother allows the daughter to work with her in the kitchen. At first she is given her own piece of pie dough to work and press into a pie tin. The miniature pie (often ending up a different color from mother's) bakes alongside the big one in the oven. Later, the child is permitted to measure out ingredients or mix the dough and roll out the crust. Before long, the daughter can make the pie without help.

Skills are learned in the pleasant companionship with Mother. Years later the daughter may look back upon these happy hours remembering the time Mother let her fry the holes in the doughnuts. (The little round balls of fried dough always taste better than the doughnuts themselves, somehow.) Junior will gleefully recall the time he came up with a solution to a problem he was working out with Dad that made Dad look at him speculatively and say: "You got something there, Son. Two heads are better than one, if one is yours."

Of course, it may well be daughter who helps Dad with the carpentering or repair of the car if there is no Junior. And it may be that Junior learns to be a pretty good cook working in the kitchen with Mother. And when he has his own family, he may gather the kids around him in the kitchen some Sunday night and say: "Your mother isn't the only good cook in this house. Let me show you how your pappy can make a batch of flapjacks," and proceed to amaze his children with his culinary skills.

When the sharing of household tasks and skills is a regular thing in a home and pride in the number of skills an individual can develop is fostered, the work that goes into running a home becomes more than just a job to do, it becomes as challenging as any game.

With this kind of training, a child soon learns that it is not only fun to know how to do any number of things, but wise too. It is a rare individual who seldom finds the opportunity to put his skills to use. The more skills he masters, the easier it is to pick up a new one as there is definite carryover value from one to another. Each new skill opens the way to new interests and pursuits of happiness. The individual with many interests never has all his eggs in one basket. If a lessening of income means that one purusit must be discontinued, he will have others just as interesting to substitute. Should illness make one type of activity impossible, the tragedy of the situation is not so great if other possibilities are available. When one has eggs in more than one basket, the loss of that basket is never so severe as when it is the only one.

The individual of many skills is less prone to do without something he wants. If he can't afford to buy something, he will try to make it. The improvised or homemade object brings joy many times. First, there is all the fun and challenge that goes into making it. Secondly, the satisfaction that comes with the phrase, "I made it myself," is hard to equal. Third, the object made with the loving care of the well-trained craftsman often surpasses the bought product which may be shoddily made to sell at a quick profit.

The Fun of Sharing Skills

It is not always the parent who teaches and the child who is on the learning end. As the children grow up and enter junior high and senior high school and acquire skills in shop, domestic science classes and electronics laboratories, it may well be that the parents will be learning from the children. Junior may know more about constructing a hi-fi set than Dad and the joys of sharing skills and knowledge will add to the fun of construction. Daughter may know how to use a new type sewing machine and will be able to do fancier tricks than Mother can do on her machine. Instead of a sewing project done by mother for daughter it may be done for mother by daughter.

The Fun of Companionship

It is always a wise parent who teaches his children at an early age that good companionship can make any activity fun, whether it be a game or household task. When the company is good and there is someone to share his experience with, any task becomes pleasant. Thus in work hours as well as play, happy family memories are accumulated and stored up to bring retrospective joy again in lonely hours just as one stores food in the fat years in anticipation of the lean years which come in every life.

Whistle While You Work

Music can gild any job and turn a dull hour into a golden one. Singing while you do the dishes takes away the drudgery and makes the job seem shorter. When two are doing the dishes together, singing rounds or songs which beg for harmony turns the work hour into playtime. Any job that is monotonous is easier when there is song. Whistling alone or with someone is fun too. People sing when they are happy. The reverse works too. If you begin singing, you'll feel happy.

Working to music on the radio or on records helps too. Ironing or scrubbing or any activity which can be done rhythmically goes faster to music. See if you can perform a particular job to music. Pushing the vacuum, sweeping the floors, dusting the furniture, is more a dance than a job if done deliberately to music.

GAMES WHILE YOU WORK

Games and dishwashing go well together, particularly puzzle and guessing games. Some games follow:

I'm Thinking of Something

This is a doing-the-dishes game. One player begins by saying: "I'm thinking of something in this room." The other player tries to discover the identity of the object by asking questions which can be answered only by "yes" or "no." For example, "Is it made of metal?" "Is it larger than I?" "Is it made from something that grew?" When the object is finally identified, the person guessing the correct answer takes his turn to think of an object. A time limit is kept for guessing on any one object. If the object has not been identified at the end of that time, the guesser must "give up" and is told the answer. The first player than takes another turn and the game begins again.

Song Guessing Game

One player whistles or sings the rhythm of a particular song in a monotone. The other player tries to guess the identity of the song from this rendition. The player guessing is told whether the song is a present-day song hit, an old-timer or musical comedy, etc. The rest is up to him. If you try this game, you'll find it is very difficult to whistle or sing a rhythm without giving away the tune.

Mystery Number Songs

One player begins: "My song has a number one in the title or words." The second player must try to identify the correct song. The songs that fit this description might be "My Wonderful One" or "Take Me Out to the Ball Game" (the "one" is in the words "and it's one, two, three strikes you're out"). When the second player identifies the song or gives up, he challenges the other player using any song and any number. One player may sing or whistle part of the tune instead of naming a song.

Mystery Song Contest

One player challenges the other to think of songs with a color in the title or lyrics. The second player is given two minutes to think of as many songs as possible (while he keeps on washing or drying the dishes, of course). When time is up, he sings or whistles or names the titles. He gets a point for each correct song. Then he challenges his opponent with another or one of the same classification. At the end of the work period, the total scores are compared and the loser pays off in some way previously agreed upon. Classifications might include boys' and girls' names, numbers, sports, countries, states, colors, rivers, flowers, trees. Some suggestion in each classification follow.

BOYS' AND GIRLS' NAMES IN SONGS

Annie	"Little Annie Rooney," "Annie Laurie," "Gentle Annie"
Augustine	"Ach Du Lieber Augustine"
Anastasia	"Anastasia"
Caroline	"Can't You Hear Me Calling Caroline?" or "Carolina Moon"
Chloe	"Chloe"
Daisy	"Daisy Belle"
Diane	"Diane"
Dinah	"Dinah," "Seeing Nellie Home"
Charmaine	"Charmaine"
Adeline	"Sweet Adeline"
Alice	"Alice Blue Gown," "Alice Ben Bolt"
Katy	"K-K-K-Katy"
Casey	"The Band Played On"
Frank or Frankie	"Frankie and Johnny"
Clementine	"Clementine"
Belle	"Daisy Belle"
Nellie	"Seeing Nellie Home," "Wait Till the Sun Shines, Nellie"
Dan	"Old Dan Tucker"
Sylvia	"Who Is Sylvia?" "Sylvia"
Joe	"Old Black Joe," "Joe Hill"
John or Johnny	"Johnny, Get Your Gun," "Oh, No, John," "Frankie and Johnny," "John Henry"
Ned	"Old Uncle Ned"
Mamie	"Sidewalks of New York"
Jeanie	"Jeanie with the Light Brown Hair"
Juanita	"Juanita"
Susie	"If You Knew Susie"
Kathleen	"I'll Take You Home Again, Kathleen"

Rose or Rosie	"Sweet Rosie O'Grady," "My Wild Irish Rose," "Mighty Lak a Rose"
Margie	"My Little Margie"
Peggy	"Peggy O'Neil"
Sally	"My Gal Sal," "Erie Canal"
David	"Little David, Play on Your Harp"

NUMBERS IN SONGS

One	"My Wonderful One"
Any number from one to ten	"Ten Little Indians"
Two	"Tea for Two"
Three	"Take Me Out to the Ball Game," "Three O'Clock in the Morning"
Four	"I'm Looking Over a Four-Leaf Clover"
Two, four or six	"I've Got Sixpence"
Fifteen	"The Erie Canal"
Sixteen	"Down by the Old Mill Stream"

SPORTS IN SONGS

Skating	"The Skaters' Waltz"
Baseball	"Take Me Out to the Ball Game"
Football	Any college football song
Rowing	"Row, Row, Row Your Boat"
Hunting	"A-Hunting We Will Go"
Camping	"Tenting on the Old Camp Ground"

COUNTRIES IN SONGS

China	"China Town, My China Town"
Japan	"Japanese Sandman"
Burma	"On the Road to Mandalay"
Italy	"Italian Street Song"
Ireland	"A Little Bit of Heaven"

STATES IN SONGS

Kentucky	"My Old Kentucky Home"
Ohio	"Beautiful Ohio"

California	"California, Here I Come"
Texas	"The Eyes of Texas Are upon You" (Tune: "I've Been Working on the Railroad")
Virginia	"Carry Me Back to Old Virginny," "The Trail of the Lonesome Pine"
New York	"Sidewalks of New York"
Missouri	"Meet Me in St. Louis"

COLORS IN SONGS AND SONG TITLES

Black	"That Old Black Magic"
Blue	"My Blue Heaven," "Blue Skies," "April Showers," "When You Wore a Tulip," "Alice Blue Gown"
Purple	"Deep Purple"
Yellow	"Carry Me Back to Old Virginny," " 'Round Her Neck She Wore a Yellow Ribbon"
White	"White Christmas," "White Cliffs of Dover"
Gray	"Old Gray Bonnet," "Little Gray Home in the West"
Red, White, Blue	"Columbia, the Gem of the Ocean"
Green	"I'll Take You Home Again, Kathleen"
Silver, Gold	"Silver Thread Among the Gold"

RIVERS IN SONGS AND SONG TITLES

Afton	"Flow Gently, Sweet Afton"
Sewanee	"Old Folks at Home"
Missouri	"Shenandoah"
Wabash	"On the Banks of the Wabash"
Mississippi	"Ol' Man River"
Jordan	"Swing Low, Sweet Chariot"
Ohio	"Beautiful Ohio"
Rhône	"On the Bridge of Avignon"
Thames	"London Bridge Is Falling Down"

FLOWERS

Rose	"My Wild Irish Rose"
Tulip	"When You Wore a Tulip"
Daisy	"Daisy Belle"
Apple blossom	"I'll Be with You in Apple Blossom Time"
Bluebell	"Bluebells Of Scotland"
Sunflower	"Believe Me If All Those Endearing Young Charms"

TREES IN SONGS

Maple	"The Maple Leaf Forever"
Mulberry	"Here We Go Round the Mulberry Bush"
Sycamore	"On the Banks of the Wabash"
Pine	"Trail of the Lonesome Pine"
Fir	"Oh, Christmas Tree" ("Tannenbaum")
Apple	"In the Shade of the Old Apple Tree"
Willow	"Oh, What a Beautiful Morning!"

Word Geography

One player begins by naming a city. The next player must come back with a city beginning with the last letter of the city previously named. A sequence might go like this: Binghamton, New Orleans, San Francisco, Orlando, Oleander, Rochester, etc. If a player cannot name a city beginning with the last letter of the previously named city, he can challenge the player who named it. Unless that player can come up with a correct answer, he loses that game. If he can, however, the second player loses the game. A new game begins after each challenge.

With older children, a time limit can be very short, no more than a minute. With younger children, a longer time limit to think can be allowed. The same time limit is allowed the player who is challenged.

Word Flowers

Play as in word geography but use names of flowers instead. A sequence might go this way: rose, everlasting, gardenia, amaryllis, sunflower, rhododendron, narcissus, snowflake and so on.

Word Trees

Play as above using names of trees. A possible sequence is: maple, elm, mulberry, yew, willow, walnut, tulip, pear, redwood, dogwood, Douglas fir and so on.

Word Names

Play as above using girls' or boys' names. Each player must name a name beginning with the last letter of the previously given name. A possible sequence is: John, Nora, Annabelle, Edwin, Noreen, Ned, Dorothy, Yaro, Octavia, Anne, Edward, etc.

Word Numbers

Play as above but allow little time between the naming of numbers. A sequence might go like this: ten, ninety-eight, twenty-seven, ninety-five. You will see as you play that there are certain numbers which end in a letter which would be impossible to follow. The next player can challenge the previous player. In the event the first player can come up with a correct answer to follow his named number the second player loses that particular game and a new game begins. If the first player cannot name a correct number, then he loses the game. For example: player calls ninety. Since there is no number beginning with a "y," the second player challenges the first and wins the game.

Given below are the letters for which numbers can be given. Players must be careful to name a number which ends in one of these letters so that the second player can continue the game.

LETTER	NUMBERS THAT CAN BE NAMED
F	Four, five, fourteen, fifteen, forty-one, forty-two, forty-three, forty-five, forty-seven, forty-eight, forty-nine, fifty-

one, and same numbers in fifties as in forties, also four hundred and one, fourteen hundred, fourteen thousand and one, etc. The numbers ending in "y" cannot be used or those ending in "r" or "x" so a four must be eliminated as well as six.

E　　　Eight, eleven, eighteen and the numbers in the eighties which do not end in "r" or "y." And numbers in the eighteen hundreds or eighteen thousands not ending in "r," "y," or "x."

O　　　One, one hundred and one or any number not ending in the tabooed letters.

N　　　Nine, ninety-one, ninety-two, -three, -five, -seven, -eight, -nine, nineteen, nineteen hundred and one, nineteen thousand and one or any of the other correct numbers.

S　　　Six, seven, sixteen, sixty-one, and any numbers in the sixties and seventies which are correct to use, any numbers in the sixteen hundreds and sixteen thousands as well as the correct numbers in the seventeen hundreds and thousands.

T　　　Ten, twenty-one and any of the correct numbers in the twenties, thirties.

You will note this is not a particularly easy game nor is it a difficult one, but the players must keep their wits about them to come up with a correct answer.

Third of a Dish Mop Game

This is a spelling game usually known as "Third of a Ghost," but the loser must wash dishes after the next meal, hence the new name.

The first player begins with any letter in the alphabet. The next player adds a letter being careful not to use a letter which will make a word. For example if the first player says "a" and the second says "n" he has made a word and loses that round making him a third of a dish mop or an "M." The first player begins a new word with the same or another letter. Each time a player finishes a word he is a third of a dish mop. When he becomes a full "MOP," he has lost that game and is in line to wash dishes the next time.

There are tricks to this game. Certain letters are difficult to follow without creating a short word. Some of these letters are "t," "m," "h," since the addition of some of the vowels immediately makes a word. To keep from ending a word, the verb tense can be changed to prolong the word. For example, a player finds himself with "tak." He could end it with "e" making "take," but he can prolong the agony by adding an "i" to make "taking." If only two players are involved the last letter will be the responsibility of the same player anyway so nothing is gained but time. If three players are involved the player adding the "i" is safe.

If a player is given a certain number of letters and cannot figure how they are making a word, he can challenge the previous player who handed him this difficult situation. The previous player must be able to name a word which is spelled in that manner or pay the forfeit and becomes a third of a mop. If he can name a word so spelled, the challenging player is then the loser of that round.

The dictionary ought to get a play with this game.

NOTE: Any of the fun-while-you-work games are also good to play as travel games in the auto, train, plane or bus.

Treasure Hunt Housecleaning

The usually arduous and distasteful job of cleaning out the attic, garage or basement can be made into a family fun project. The job is set for a particular day and notice is served that nothing short of a broken leg excuses any member of the family from participating. A family conference is called. The various duties are assigned at this advance session so each knows what is expected of him. From the smallest to the eldest there is some special responsibility assigned. The necessary cleaning equipment and the plan of operation are laid out like a battle campaign. The on-the-job time is definitely set. Coffee and Coke break time is put on the schedule.

On the appointed day, the family assembles at the scheduled hour and each goes to work at his appointed task. Where does the treasure hunt come in? In the process of cleaning up, two piles of stuff are made—the junk pile and the treasure pile. Bottles which bring a deposit return when taken to the store, old metal or paper which can be sold, long-lost articles which miraculously appear all go on the treasure pile. All other junk is sorted as to rubbish that is burnable and that which is not. (Beware of workers who surreptitiously attempt to transfer rubbish to the treasure pile or nothing will ever be thrown away!) The proceeds from all salable articles go to the kids and are equally divided among them. Therein lies the treasure. In no time at all a job that might have been a chore for any one person is quickly dispensed with. To everybody's surprise it was more fun than work.

Snow Shoveling Fun

Every winter brings one or two heavy snowfalls which are enough to break one shoveler's back or, worse, give someone a heart attack. Such a job if made into a family fun project gets done faster and is more fun than a party.

Everyone gets into his snow clothes and armed with shovels and brooms and anything that will remove snow goes out bravely to the fight. With everyone shoveling and with time out occasionally for the horseplay that develops under such circumstances, the drive and sidewalks are soon cleared. Mom who has disappeared a few minutes before the job is finished greets the red-nosed, apple-cheeked family with steaming cups of hot chocolate and plates of cinnamon toast. A hard job has been turned into an occasion for family fun long to be remembered. Once again the family proves it is as much fun working as playing together.

Garden Clean-up and Spading Time

In spring and fall the garden and yard need a lot of work done in a relatively short time. In spring the debris which has collected during the winter must be raked up, the garden plot needs spading, the rubbish and weeds need burning. For one person this is a hard job. When the whole family attacks the job at once, each with his own particular task, the job gets finished in a hurry. Fun time comes when wieners and hamburgers are broiled over the red embers of the rubbish fire.

In fall the leaf-raking duties need more than one pair of hands. The reward at the end of this task (which is a pleasant one when the whole family works together) is the privilege of jumping into and rolling around in the pile of accumulated leaves before they are burned or boxed awaiting their removal by the rubbish collectors. A time-out break for a surprise treat of ice cream bars or soft drinks and cookies does no harm.

These are only a few of the kinds of jobs which need to be done around any home and which can be turned into family fun fests.

Bibliography

Halstead, Homer, *How to Live in the Woods*. Boston: Little, Brown and Co., 1948.

Ledlie, John A., *Handbook of Trail Campcraft*. New York: Association Press, 1954.

Swanson, William E., *Camping for All It's Worth*. New York: The Macmillan Company, 1952.

Weaver, Robert W., and Merrill, Anthony F., *Camping Can Be Fun*. New York: Harper & Brothers, 1948.

Zarchy, Harry, *Let's Go Camping*. New York: Alfred A. Knopf, 1951.

Zeligs, Dorothy F., *The Story of Jewish Holidays and Customs*. New York: Bloch Publishing Co., 1951.

MISCELLANEOUS

Audubon Nature Bulletins. Series 4 #7, Series 7 #4, Series 14 #1, Series 15 #8, Series 16 #8, Series 19 #1, Series 21 #4, Series 22 #2.

Mulac, Margaret E., *Recreation: Its Role in Education for Retirement* (Thesis Submitted in Partial Fulfillment for Requirements for Degree of Master of Arts). Western Reserve University, 1953.

Index

251

Set in linotype Garamond No. 3
Format by Joe Vesely
Manufactured by The Riverside Press
Published by HARPER & BROTHERS, *New York*